0/18

£3

ON THE LONELY SHORE

Don Whyte

On the Lonely Shore

An autobiography

Foreword
by Hugh MacDiarmid

Hutchinson of London

Hutchinson & Co (Publishers) Ltd
3 Fitzroy Square, London W1

London Melbourne Sydney Auckland
Wellington Johannesburg and agencies
throughout the world

First published 1977
© Don Whyte 1977

Set in Monotype Baskerville

Printed in Great Britain by
The Anchor Press Ltd and bound by
Wm Brendon & Son Ltd
both of Tiptree, Essex

ISBN 0 09 128800 2

This book is especially dedicated to Anne. It is also for the many people who bothered to pick me up when I fell down.

There is a pleasure in the pathless woods,
There is a rapture on the lonely shore,
There is society, where none intrudes,
By the deep sea, and music in its roar:
I love not man the less, but Nature more,
From these our interviews, in which I steal
From all I may be, or have been before,
To mingle with the Universe, and feel
What I can ne'er express, yet cannot all conceal.

Byron: *Childe Harold*

Contents

Illustrations

Acknowledgements

I am grateful to the *Scottish Daily Express* for kindly supplying copies of several of the photographs and to the editor for giving me permission to include these in this book.

Foreword
by Hugh MacDiarmid

This book is personal journalism of a kind rare today – perhaps always rare. Most writers about nature and the environment, about sailing, mountaineering and so forth, attempt to write them up – above the spoken voice as it were – whereas Don Whyte writes exactly as he would speak on such things if he were reminiscing to a group of friends.

His own character is the basic element. Those who know him personally, and know something of his life, will realize that the astonishing thing about this book, and about all the journalistic work he has done over a long period of years, is simply that it has been done at all.

Stricken by polio in boyhood, he has had to struggle ever since against physical handicap, and it is a marvel that he has kept going without being soured in any way or permitting any element of bitterness or self-pity in his work. He has contrived to lead a very full life, journeying all over Scotland – enriching it with a love for the people he has encountered, and constantly replenished with fresh delight in his surroundings. It is a remarkable achievement to all but himself, for he seems unconscious of it and takes it all as just part of his day's work.

Don is the son of the late Dr Ian Whyte, who was music director of the BBC in Scotland, and no doubt derives much of his love of Scotland from his father. But he has widened his appreciation of Scotland and Scottish life through the sweetness and abundant zest of his own personality. That is why his articles in the *Scottish Daily Express* are appreciated all over the country.

Fifty years ago I wrote that a great improvement was becoming discernible in books about Scotland. Norman Douglas, Neil Gunn and George Scott Moncrieff are among those writers who, in recent years, have done splendid work. Yet most of them lack something that is at the very heart of Don Whyte's book. It is the subtleties which rule in all his work, differentiating it from that of other journalists. There is never anything second-hand, never any failure of interest and delight. Every sentence in his book rings true. He is sharing his life with his readers in a way few writers can do, and it is a life supremely worth having, not to escape *from* our troubled world, but *into* it.

I

Sammy Side-pooches

The dormer window of my birthplace looked northwards across the Aberdeenshire Dee. The river itself was screened from view by trees at the foot of our garden, but I think I was always aware of its existence.

On a night of cathedral calm when owls murmured in the woods, a sudden sough of air would carry the river noise to my listening ears. Sometimes it sounded like people talking incessantly, earnestly arguing about nothing in particular, but never out of temper. In times of spate the voices deepened and roughened, bellowed and shouted abuse. But these quarrels never seemed to last for long: rivers are easier to live with than many people.

Beyond the Dee and the town of Aboyne the gentle cone of Mortlich stood against the horizon, mauve against blue under summer heath, white against blue-grey under the snows of winter. What it looked like in spring and autumn I cannot recall; for during my calf days there were only two seasons to any year.

Summer was a rhapsody of warm lawn grass and the smell of ripening strawberries. Summer was when honey-suckle clung to our porch of spaniel brown, and its scent clung to my nostrils. Summer was a plethora of sweet-peas and peonies, a nuzzling of bees, a guzzling of raspberries and farm cream and gooseberry fool. There were currants to pick and jams and jellies to make. You might say that I had come to a sticky beginning – but my fourth summer nearly brought me to a similar end.

Our solid cottage of granite was called Millbank, standing

as it did a few yards from a sawmill's black and shiny pond. By standing on tiptoe I could peer over our garden wall and marvel.

Green trees lay drowsing on the jet mirror, and sometimes a white duck would smash the black glass and shatter the reflected leaves into a myriad emeralds. Swallows skimmed there, and damsel flies of dazzling azure hovered among the reeds.

I was entranced – and Mother knew it. Never was I to go near the pond. 'If you do,' she warned, 'you will fall in, and slimy eels will wrap themselves round your legs and drag you under.'

This deterrent worked pretty well for a while. But there came the famous day that my romper suit was laid away and I was given a real shirt and real boy's trousers. So the butterfly sloughed his chrysalis and went to spread his wings in the sunlight.

There were men working on the cottage roof. 'Man, laddie – you're fairly grown up noo!' one of them greeted my début.

My pride knew no bounds. It had taken me four interminable years to reach this status of manhood. I strutted and I swaggered, stuck hands in my crisp new pockets; and the men cheered me on.

When they seemed to lose interest, I determined to put on an even more impressive display. The garden wall was surprisingly easy to climb. A narrow path ran along the edge of the pond. I marched down it like a bantam cock, and I think I must have swung round to assess audience reaction. Whatever the reason, my warm world of sunlight and self-esteem turned abruptly to a cold hell of dark water and terror.

I managed to grasp a tussock of grass and hang on. The workmen were no longer in view, and I must have whimpered for a moment or two. I might have cried out and not been heard. I could have drowned. But a worse horror was in store – one which probably saved my arrogant young life.

Even now I can feel the ghastly writhing as something, colder than pond water and far slimier, coiled its loathsomeness lovingly around my bare legs. In all likelihood it was a frond of weed. But my mind shrieked 'Eels!' – and somehow I was out of that pond quicker than I had fallen in.

I remember my sobbing, sodden return along the path and over the wall, the hoots of laughter from the roof, the ignominy of being stripped and scolded in front of Mother's daily help (her name was, of all things, Mrs Triptree) and the reappearance of my romper suit with its pearl buttons and embroidered pockets. Thus attired I was sent out to face the world.

Yells of masonic laughter greeted me. The final insult descended from above clothed in a phrase I have never forgotten: 'Haw – look at Sammy Side-pooches!'

So manhood ended and childhood days began in grim earnest. Recollections of these early days are sporadic. They do not roll continuously like a cine film: the young mind takes snapshots mostly in moments of high drama.

I remember vividly seeing aircraft for the first time. Two biplanes they were, droning up the Dee Valley like horizontal ladders in the sky: their noise sent me running to the cottage in terror. I remember the shock of falling downstairs; of seeing Winnie, our Airedale, being run over by a car; of jumping among old planks and impaling my foot on a large nail. I also remember my first spanking, soundly administered by Father in the stick-shed.

'Never . . . never . . . ever . . . do . . . a . . . thing . . . like . . . that . . . again,' he intoned, accompanying himself with the flat of his hand on my bare bottom.

To this day I cannot remember committing the actual crime. But being reminded of it in later years filled me – and still fills me – with a sense of awe. I had threatened a small girl with a hatchet, which is wicked enough in anyone's book of social behaviour.

But to have selected as victim the child destined to become First Lady of the land was pushing villainy to the extreme.

Deeside in the late 1920s was even more Royal than it is today. The farther upstream one went towards Balmoral, the more regal it seemed to become. Aboyne and Ballater oozed with dowagers and land-locked admirals, honourables and venerables. Even the salmon, I think, wore insignia instead of spots. But tourism had not yet hemmed in nobility behind its wrought iron gates. Informality was still possible.

And so to the lane adjoining our back garden one afternoon came children in care of a nanny. Father recognized one pretty face – that of Elizabeth, daughter of the Duke of York. They were going fishing on the loch behind our cottage, the nanny explained, and might they have some worms? Father found an old tin and his graip and began to dig. Apparently the sight of other children claiming his attention and usurping my territory aroused the robin in me: I rushed to the attack. . . .

I like today to think that I inspired no great or lasting panic. I like to think that the victim of my jealous rage has forgotten the incident as her assailant has forgotten it (his spanking apart). Or if some glimmering remains of a summer day more than forty years ago, may it help both majesty and humility to the understanding that it is even possible to influence history by digging for worms in a midden. If our Queen has forgotten her fishing excursion at least her loyal subject remembers the stick-shed.

We were not an aggressive family by nature, but even my father came close to outraging law and order when circumstances forced him to take up arms against a marauding hare. This animal took a penchant for his cabbages and, despite wire netting and flailing arms, arrived each evening to nibble a path of devastation through the brassica. Father, who abominated firearms, finally borrowed a powerful air rifle from a friend in the village and lay in wait at an upstairs window. As dusk was falling the hare came lolloping to his banquet. Father took shaky aim and fired. The slug struck a stone and riccocheted. The hare fled and the evening was enlivened by the sound of tinkling glass.

On the other side of our lane there lived Miss Jamieson, an elderly and formidable relic of Victorian days. She wore, I recall, a long, grey skirt with a sparse beard to match and spent most of her time sitting on a stool plucking weeds from the cracks in her crazy paving. But on this particular evening she was doing what no Victorian lady ever dared to admit.

As she perched on the throne of necessity the opaque glass of her bathroom window shattered and an air-gun slug dropped at her feet. There had been a deliberate attempt made to assassinate her, she told the village constable. And in due course he arrived at our door.

'Is Mr Whyte at home?' he asked my mother.

'I'm afraid not,' she lied. 'Can I help you instead?'

He asked if firearms were kept in the house, and Mother was horrified. 'Goodness no,' she said. 'My husband loathes guns and shooting.' And in this she was telling the truth.

The policeman attributed the incident to some boyish prank and went his way. My father emerged from hiding and fearfully, at dead of night, returned the rifle to its owner. No more was heard of the matter and thereafter the hare dined in peace.

Sometime later Father brought me a toy glider from Aberdeen. It was silver and blue, I remember, and had its nose weighted with lead. With infinite care he trimmed wings and tail for flight and hooked it to its catapult. With breathtaking grace it circled our garden, gaining height in some thermal until the God who loves small boys, hares and Miss Jamiesons intervened. Above the lane it hesitated – and then plunged like an arrow towards a certain newly-glazed bathroom window.

I was surprised when Father dragged me indoors and bitterly disappointed when he refused to retrieve my glider. For days it reposed in a tree close to Miss Jamieson's throne room, unnoticed by her and mourned by myself. I did not then understand that when a man has recently failed to shoot an old lady he is at pains to keep dark any suggestion of having launched a subsequent aircraft attack. My glider stayed there until the wind blew it out of sight like a winged seed to flourish only in the good soil of memory.

Excursions to the village were fairly infrequent and were mostly made to buy meat and bread, barley and oatmeal. We did not need – or perhaps could not afford – to do much shopping. Our milk and eggs came from the Murdochs' farm at the foot of the road, and our garden was a place of plenty throughout the year. Only occasionally had Mother to ask if we would like some special titbit.

'Let's have curtains,' I suggested one day; and this, of course, was asking for trouble.

My father gave my mother one of those slant-eyed Chinese looks, used by psychologists when the patient exhibits signs of dementia.

I was told not to be so silly, and the matter was forgotten until our next visit to the village. We were passing the shop of Dinnie the butcher when I beheld him holding up lengths of white stuff for a customer's inspection.

'Curtains,' I cried. And Mother, following my pointing finger, burst into laughter.

'That,' she explained, 'is called tripe.' But for many a day to come curtains continued to play a substantial part in our diet.

Mother was a superb cook. Her country upbringing had taught her the virtues of economy and invention. Under her skilled hand a joint of meat took on the role of a character actor, appearing first as himself, and then assuming so many successive guises that we forgot his original identity. To open a tin was little short of sinful. The milk and honey of my childhood flowed direct from byre and hive with no intervening process.

And as Mother cooked and baked in our kitchen with its black iron range she was persistently attended (and often infuriated) by an assistant chef whose name was Dick.

Every garden, they say, has its own robin. But not every robin has its own garden and cottage complete with larder, hot water system and other avian conveniences. Dick was one of the élite, the sole proprietor of Millbank; and we were his mere tenants. My parents had the habit of sleeping with their bedroom window slightly open at the top. Even an inch sufficed to let Dick squeeze in, usually at daybreak when unfeathered adults are not at their best and brightest.

From his perch on the bedpost he would sing, splintering sleep to pieces with a fusillade of needle-sharp notes. Unless someone got up fairly smartly he would decorate his perch with his personal insignia, but if the bedroom door were open he would fly downstairs to breakfast. No matter how carefully my parents closed doors and windows, Dick always seemed to gain admittance to butter, cheese and fat. Our familiar was utterly contemptuous.

He sat on one haft of the spade while my father's foot

delved with the other, riding out a storm of digging until the worm of his choice appeared. He perched on the rim of my mother's baking bowl until the desired raisin surfaced on her spoon. A quick stab of the beak and he was off.

Sometimes he perched the wrong way on her mixing bowl, adding guano to self-raising flour and the last straw to her industrious back. One flick of her spoon removed the excrement. Repeated swipes at Dick with her dish-cloth only served to accelerate his progress from room to room. His final refuge was inevitably a crevice between our hot water pipes where he fluffed himself out into unassailable sentimentality with one black eye half shut and the other firmly focussed on the butter.

Dick, we knew, was married; but how often, fondly or loosely we never found out. In April, when his visits were least frequent, Father would follow him from the garden into a wilderness of tangled leafage locally called the Fungle – but never found his nest. Only the occasional beakful of food, harvested from our larder, suggested that in the shade of some secret thicket there were other mouths to feed. Once and once only did another robin follow him into our house. It might have been his mate or his eldest unmarried son, but recognition was made impossible. The interloper vanished in a maelstrom of whirling feathers leaving Dick in sole charge of his immovable estate. He had even the cheek to chivvy me on my way to school for the first time, only stopping short in a bush at that invisible line where his territory and mine ended and the rest of the world began.

I had dreaded going to school, that austere building which lay in wait beside the village green. I had passed it often enough before (holding my mother's hand) and had observed its two distinct moods: the one an ominous brooding of heads over desks, and the other an indescribable mêlée called play-time. To an only child of five both punishments seemed unnecessary and undeserved. But Mother deposited me firmly on the threshold of learning with a quaking heart, an empty satchel, a piece of bread and butter and an apple.

.   .   .   .   .

Miss Clark was our teacher. Along with some thirty slightly larger children I watched fascinated, as she took a piece of red chalk and drew a large A on the blackboard.

'Aaaa-y,' she sang. 'The first big letter we have to think about is Aaaa-y. Everybody say Aaaa-y.'

What there was to think about heaven alone knows. But we all said Aaaa-y in chorus. By the time she got round to Beee, written in blue, and Ceee in yellow, half an hour had elapsed and I was beginning to grow bored. I started to write on my slate and Miss Clark was not slow to notice. She advanced upon me carefully, like a cat crossing a mantelshelf of ornaments.

'Are you drawing something nice?' she asked me sweetly. In an agony of self-consciousness, I allowed her to inspect my work. Intrigued perhaps more by the squeak of the pencil than by the methods of Scottish primary education, I had written the alphabet from A to Z and had decorated it with an airship and an elephant, neither of which appeared conversant with the third dimension.

Miss Clark seemed more than satisfied. She stuck a lump of plasticene in front of me with an encouraging smile. She said: 'Since you seem to know your ABC so well, you may play with this.'

My classmates scowled their displeasure, and my large and ugly ears burned with embarrassment. It was apparently all my fault that I had learned to read and write at the age of three, and had earned the right to amuse myself while everyone else was slaving.

I cannot remember learning anything new at Aboyne school except that A is red, B blue, C yellow, D brown, E grey, F mauve and so on – right down to Z which is white. Even today the colours of the alphabet are quite distinct in my mind. My first school book failed to impress me, because it made reading so infernally complicated and took so long to impart what little it had to say.

'Jack is a lit-tle boy. Jill is his lit-tle sis-ter. Is not Jack a lucky boy to have a lit-tle sis-ter?' was the kind of deathless prose contained in its pages. And so I did most of my reading at home.

One of my favourite books was a fat tome called the

Mickey Mouse Annual, and one of its better passages is still firmly entrenched in my mind.

> *Mickey had a little lamp*
> *He filled it with benzene,*
> *He went to light that little lamp*
> *And for days he's not benzene.*

It was perhaps from this masterpiece that I derived a lasting affection for the pun, a kind of disease known as paronomasia, which put the ancient Greeks beside themselves with laughter.

At playtime on my first morning at school I retired to a quiet corner to eat my bread and apple. But I had been observed. A boy, larger than I, with lank yellow hair and a sheep's face advanced on me threateningly.

'Gi'es a bite yer eppul,' he said; and although the language sounded foreign to my ears there was no mistaking its meaning. Obediently I handed over my apple. Sheep-face took an enormous slobbery bite and handed it back. I looked at it in dismay and, when his back was turned, sadly consigned it to the litter basket.

The language spoken by my playmates fascinated me. At home I had been encouraged to speak plain English, and shielded from what Mother called coarse speech. But here was a thrilling new experience. My contemporaries called school 'squeal'. Boys were loons and girls quines. 'Feet' meant 'what' and 'gweed' was 'good'. Bit by bit I mastered this delightful tongue, and pretty soon I was able to regale Mother with such choice expressions as 'feet time is't?' (what time is it?) and 'far's the bit duggie?' (where is the little dog?). Mother shared Queen Victoria's lack of amusement: she treated my new-found language rather like a horse, free to achieve expression in the field but on no account to be allowed in the house. I think she was relieved that my Aberdeen-shire schooling lasted less than a year, a sentiment which at the time I did not share.

Her final disillusionment came one afternoon in 1931. She had left Millbank as usual to collect her offspring when, on the fringe of the village green, she espied two small vermilion figures walking towards her. I think that thoughts of dwarves ran in her mind, for her footsteps slowed as she approached. She finally stopped altogether, her eyes fixed as if hypnotized. 'Hello, Mummy,' I said, and the spell was broken.

My pal and I had discovered a pot of red lead under-coating complete with brush. Quite solemnly I had painted him, beginning correctly at the top with his hair, and working steadily downwards to cover shirt, jacket, trousers, stockings and boots. And with this accomplished to our mutual satisfaction it seemed only fitting that my friend should perform the same obligement for me. My God, we looked beautiful!

What his mother said and did when he got home I never learned. All I know is that by the time my mother had dragged me to the cottage, wind and sun and body heat had dried my red coating fairly hard. Mrs Triptree's Pekingese eyes (I think the soul suffered from goitre) bulged more than ever. Mother set to work on me with a blunt knife, turpentine and a scrubbing brush. The pain and its duration made spanking totally unnecessary, and the reappearance of the dreaded romper suit, now much too small, pruned me right back down to size. It was not very long after this that we left Aboyne for Edinburgh.

2

The Facts of Life

How I came to Aboyne in the first place, who I was and, more important, why, were questions which used to puzzle me. Even as late as 1930 – in Deeside at least – women were incapable of *having* children: they simply stumbled upon them by accident, having first acquired a husband capable of earning enough to feed and clothe them. Sexual reproduction was not, so far as I understand, invented until several years later.

My aunt for example, had not far to search for her two daughters. Both were discovered conveniently under gooseberry bushes in her garden. Perhaps for this reason she harboured the delusion that I too had been found in similar circumstances. I was always at pains to tell her the facts of life. For Mother had often recounted the true story of my discovery. Father and she had been ascending the Devil's Elbow in their Galloway coupé one wintery evening. A blizzard was blowing and visibility poor when they noticed a small pink thing crawling by the roadside clothed only in a vest.

'I picked you up in my arms,' her saga ended, 'and wrapped you up in a big cosy shawl. We took you home to a warm fire, fed you and tucked you up in bed – and we've kept you ever since.'

The effect of this recital was to induce copious tears of compassion and self-pity. Not until I was seven or eight years old did I begin to doubt Mother's veracity, being led by children more worldly wise to abandon romantic fiction for prosaic fact.

But the story of how my parents met and married is far from prosaic. Considering the circumstances, it sometimes seems to me incredible that I contrived to make my appearance in the world at all.

Father was born in Crossford village, on the western outskirts of Dunfermline. His maternal grandfather was the village smith, a craftsman of considerable skill who numbered fiddle-making among his accomplishments. The clamour of hammer on anvil and the frisk of the fiddle, my father claimed, were the first sounds of music he could remember. His own parents both sang, and were in frequent demand at concerts and soirées in the district. When he himself acquired a precocious appetite for music they saw to it that he did not go hungry. Handel's Messiah was the family bible, whose score he was able to read, and reproduce tolerably at the piano, by the age of six.

When he was ten he was given his first professional engagement. The organist of Dalmeny Kirk, across the Forth Rail Bridge, had become indisposed. Apparently no competent adult could be found to deputize, and the choice fell on young Ian. It is not on record what the congregation thought as he made his short-trousered début in the organ loft, but Father was pretty furious. Although conversant with the principle of organ pedals, he found that his legs were too short to reach them – and had to make do with the manuals. He was better pleased at the end of morning service to pocket his fee of five shillings.

As a pupil of Dunfermline High School he somehow managed to learn some Latin, Greek and mathematics; for much of his time in class was spent in the furtive scribbling of music.

He did not particularly enjoy school games. His preoccupation with music stuck out like an organ stop and made him the butt of the playground. This he managed to tolerate until one enterprising youth sneaked up behind him one day and kicked him hard and painfully on the coccyx. Father punched him, just once, breaking his assailant's jaw. The incident brought him within an inch of expulsion – but served to teach his schoolmates some respect for the finer arts.

The First World War broke out when he was thirteen, at

which time my mother was manageress of a restaurant in Dunfermline. HMS *Lion* and *Tiger* and other men-of-war were at the neighbouring naval base of Rosyth. Mother was asked to organize a party for officers and ratings and wondered what entertainment she could lay on. Someone suggested Ian Whyte, a local lad and a talented pianist, and with some hesitation she agreed to try him out.

He arrived, slightly unkempt, and her first painful duty was to ask him to go and wash his hands. Of such strange encounters romance is born. Father's performance passed muster – but it did not end with his final party piece. He took the opportunity to fall violently in love, and spent the next ten years brooking no refusal in his dogged determination to lead Mother to the altar.

A Dunfermline Carnegie Trust Scholarship took him to the Royal College of Music in London where he studied under Stanford. And London might seem to have been the most fruitful place in which to begin a musical career, but Mother and Scotland were powerful magnets. Opportunities north of Tweed were few. In the pre-1928 era of silent films he earned a pittance as a cinema pianist, extemporizing to suit the mood of the film.

A music seller in Glasgow eventually employed him as a demonstrator to prospective piano buyers. But marriage seemed a distant hope until a chance meeting brightened his whole horizon.

Into the shop one day walked a man scarcely his senior who listened attentively while Father was playing and finally got into conversion with him. Father, who never tolerated fools gladly, was impressed by the stranger's obvious musicality. Impressions were mutual; for the encounter quickly blossomed into friendship, and friendship into alliance.

Thomas Coats, the late Baron Glentanar, was a man of taste, himself a pianist and organist of some ability. His burning ambition at the time was to stage opera at Glentanar House on his estate near Aboyne; to recruit performers from among his house guests and such local people as might be persuaded to take part. There was moreover the vacancy for the post of organist at St Thomas's Episcopal Church in the village. Would my father be interested?

He required, I think, little coaxing. However this adventure might turn out, it was certainly preferable to helping to sell pianos to fusty customers who couldn't tell B flat from a bull's foot. It also made marriage a viable prospect.

My parents were married at Amulree, the wild little Perthshire hamlet where Mother's uncle owned the hotel, and where she herself had spent much of her young womanhood. As might be expected where a man of Father's temperament was concerned the nuptials did not pass without their anxious moments. When the wedding guests had assembled in church, and when the bride was ready to make her appearance, the bridegroom was nowhere to be found.

Ordered to satisfy superstition by keeping his eyes off his intended, he had taken the opportunity to go fishing. Having no watch, he had no idea of the hour. A hasty search of moorland and peat hags discovered him attired in tweeds and trout scales. A frantic cross-country, a wash and a quick change allowed the marriage to proceed as planned.

But Mother, I imagine, had already seen the writing on the wall (the glint in the river is perhaps a better phrase) for in the Aberdeenshire days to come, and for long afterwards, there were many hours in which the scherzo of hill water proved more irresistible than the slow movement of domesticity. Music and fishing were the consuming interests of Father's life, the one seeming strangely to complement the other.

I remember little of his musical activities at Aboyne, but I vividly recall his homecomings from the Tanar Water with trout freckled black and crimson over old gold, and sometimes seatrout with ocean silver minted on their sides.

In 1930 he was offered the Musical Directorship of the BBC in Scotland, and in the following year we left for Edinburgh.

The last winter we spent at Aboyne was the worst I can remember. It began one evening as we drove home from Aberdeen in Father's sedate and elderly Daimler. Snow rode on the back of a galloping gale and began to thicken and drift on the Deeside road. At one point a fallen tree blocked our path, small enough fortunately for my father and another motorist to drag aside. But as they laboured, a gust of wind ripped the canvas hood from our car, and a long wet chase ensued before it could be retrieved.

Our journey ended in a three-foot snow drift at the bottom of our lane. Mother and I waded home while Father went to enlist the help of Mr Murdoch's draught horses. In our black kitchen the range fire was dead and there were paraffin lamps to trim and light. That night, I swear, the cold was something one could smell. A faint whimper caught Mother's ear and she opened the back door. The chaos which followed I shall never forget.

An avalanche of snow hurtled in upon us, knocking us off our feet, and in the midst lay old Winnie, frozen stiff but still alive. The door of the garage, where her bed was, had slammed shut in the blizzard, locking her out. Patiently she had lain at the back door awaiting our return while six feet of snow drifted over her. We had to thaw her out with hot water bottles.

A small chirrup made us look up, and there on his favourite water pipes sat Dick, fluffed out like a feather duster. Although all windows and doors had been closed on our departure for Aberdeen, he had still managed to find his way in. Despite the cold we made quite a family party that night. But it was the last of its kind.

Winnie, my parents felt, was too old and too thralled to country ways to take kindly to living in a city. As if to prove them wrong she had an affair with a black Labrador and produced six pups on my mother's birthday. The disposal of livestock seemed to occupy our last Aboyne days. Winnie herself had ultimately to be put to sleep but, thankfully, I was not told at the time.

My real heartbreak came after Mother had spotted a mouse in the larder. A trap was set, baited with cheese; but nothing happened for a day or two. It was the faithful Mrs Triptree who heard the snap of the spring and sang out that the mouse had been caught. And how I wish she had been right.

Mother ran to investigate with myself in hot pursuit. In the trap lay Dick, having forced an entry for the last time, his breast a deeper red in death than it had been in life. For the first time Mother held him in her hands and tried to

27

rekindle that tiny fire. But by then he would be squeezing through a chink in some Elysian window. . . .

With Dick there seemed to fly away something of the very essence of childhood, the sparkle and fun of sun and frost. A well-loved nursery rhyme became utterly unbearable to my ears. The lamentations of all the birds of the air were as nothing compared to mine. The grey arms of Edinburgh reached out in cold embrace.

3

My Lady Edinburgh

My first impression of Edinburgh was one of grimness and grime. Our cottage at Aboyne had been built of granite which, even on a dull day, winked a myriad eyes of quartz and mica and stayed unsullied. Even in the city of Aberdeen the bloom of granite seemed impervious to the bad breath of industry.

But the powdered pores of my lady Edinburgh's complexion were clogged with greasy soot. It was impossible to touch stone, tree or railing without being smeared with it. I thought the city pretty disgraceful, and it did not surprise me that grown-ups, when they wanted to look smart, attired themselves in greys and blacks.

Much of Edinburgh appeared to be built on the edge of cliffs – and in grave danger of falling off. If you stood in Princes Street and looked at the castle when a north wind was blowing, its roofs and battlements threatened to topple from their rock on to the railway line beneath. The illusion, of course, was created by the southerly drift of clouds, but it was new to a boy whose mind was barely cottage-high.

Our first home in Edinburgh was a flat in Randolph Cresent – flat only in the sense that, after an ascent of tortuous stairs, it levelled out into an eyrie overlooking a canyon of the Water of Leith. Lord Randolph, I was told, was a hero who dared to lead his men up Edinburgh's central eminence to storm the castle at the top. Subsequently he had performed a leap across the water, no doubt thrilling his credulous chroniclers, but leaving their readers baffled as to how the feat was accomplished without the help of spring-heeled boots. I had cause later to regret ever having heard of his exploits.

In Edinburgh it now became a matter of some urgency for my father to acquire a good piano. The old upright he had had at Aboyne was no longer adequate for his requirements, and it was my mother, by haunting salerooms, who discovered a suitable instrument. It was a magnificent full grand Bechstein cased in rosewood. She telephoned Father:

'Come and see this piano as quickly as you can. But when you try it out remember to play badly,' she said.

By the time he arrived a small crowd of people had gathered for the auction. Father sat down and began to play, remembering one of his party tricks. This consisted in his playing 'Colonel Bogey' in B flat with the right hand, and harmonizing with the left in the key of A. This cacophonous arrangement he entitled 'The Cowdenbeath Brass Band' – which was possibly a gross insult to the musicians of that town, but the effect was devastating.

His audience screwed up their faces in horror, blamed the Bechstein instead of its assailant, and drifted away. The piano was knocked down to my parents for £35, but their adventure had not quite ended.

The auctioneers agreed to provide labour and transport to instal the monster in our house. A whole posse of men arrived and began to manoeuvre its gigantic frame upstairs. The scene which ensued came straight from Laurel and Hardy. On the turn of our stair the piano stuck, imprisoning removers and neighbours at the top and rendering impossible any access or assistance from below. In desperation Father contacted a firm of piano dealers who sent down a couple of experts to view the situation. To the discomfiture of the removal men, brawn was waved aside to make room for brain, and our piano was installed in a matter of minutes.

I was really embarrassed when my parents sent me to a girls' school in Abercrombie Place. The fact that it was also a preparatory school for boys did nothing to lessen my apprehension. And not until I found other boys of my own age in the same class did I feel mollified. Bigger girls, I discovered too, were not such awful creatures: they tended to be sweet and motherly – and even interesting; for at the age of seven I was already beginning to be aware of the vague twitterings and buzzings of the birds and the bees.

From St Serf's, as it was called, I was sent to George Watson's College for Boys, and my education began with a bang. A little late for class on my first day there, not knowing my way around, I ran along a passageway and was confronted by a military-looking man in blue uniform.

His cropped iron-grey hair and moustaches bristled. 'Hold out your hand,' he commanded.

I don't know that I exactly expected a handshake or a present. What I did not expect was the swish of a Lochgelly and the cutting pain of its thongs across my palm. Not knowing what crime I had committed worsened the hurt and I entered a classroom of strangers in an agony of shame and tears. I had found out the hard way that running in the corridors was a punishable offence, and that the janitor had full authority to uphold the law.

Football, the game I loved, was tolerated only in our quadrangle at playtime, when as many as seven or eight games would be played simultaneously on the same asphalt pitch. The confusion was unimaginable. It was not uncommon to find the road to goal blocked by fourteen full backs and half-a-dozen goalies. And that we actually managed to score in that mêlée was surely proof of our skill.

Rugby was compulsory, and a game I loathed to play. I had neither the weight and muscle to be aggressive, nor the temperament to endure hurt. My only attribute was fleetness of foot, and I was put out to graze (in each sense of the word) at wing-threequarter. My rugby career ended at Inverleith Park when our 10th fifteen was scheduled to play the corresponding team from Daniel Stewart's, and I was fielded at full-back.

Imagine my horror when an opposing side of giants trotted on to the pitch. Chickenpox, or some such seasonal pastime, had precluded the appearance of Stewart's 10th team and their 7th had kindly agreed to deputize. In vain I attempted to stem a flood of striped jerseys. In vain I tried to shield my person from remorseless knees and boots. I lost count of the tally against us when it was somewhere in the high sixties.

An inspection of my shattered remains convinced my

parents that ludo was safer. They approached the school authorities, and thereafter I was excused blood sports. I really was an appalling softie. Somehow or other I contrived to become athletic in other fields. I liked cricket because it was, contrary to Scottish belief, one of the fastest games going, demanding electric reflexes and a nice balance between hand, foot and eye.

I learned to swim and to play a kind of hacking, untutored golf. Rugby had already taught me that fleetness of foot was the essence of self-survival: it was therefore hardly surprising that I excelled as a sprinter. Long-distance running was beyond the capacity of my skinny chest.

On the academic side I seemed to do reasonably well. English presented no great difficulties, and arithmetic was a straightforward bore. History I enjoyed more than most as I had a strange facility for remembering dates. The only year I could never remember was the one in which Columbus discovered America – thanks to a silly schoolboy joke.

Teacher: 'When did Columbus discover America, Johnny?'

Johnny: 'Please miss, I don't know.'

Teacher: 'Use this simple little rhyme and you will never forget. "In fourteen-hundred and ninety-two Columbus crossed the ocean blue."'

Asked the same question by his teacher the next day, Johnny replied: 'In fourteen-hundred and ninety-three Columbus crossed the deep blue sea.' To this day I still have to look up a textbook to make certain which is correct. Memory is a fickle creature. When I was ten I sat an exam we called the 'Qually' – a kind of pre-war eleven-plus designed to prove our suitability for senior education.

The first question on the English paper ordered us to analyse the following:

To men of other minds my fancy flies,
Embosom'd in the deep where Holland lies.
Methinks her patient sons before me stand
Where the broad ocean leans against the land,
And, sedulous to stop the coming tide,
Lift the tall rampart's artificial pride.

(Goldsmith)

I made no conscious effort at the time to memorize these rather high-flown lines, and I have never come across them since. The mere chore of analysis was sufficient to engrave them in my mind forever. I only wish that passages of greater moment had embedded themselves so easily.

As might be expected my parents entertained the cosy hope that I would show an early aptitude for music, but in this they were due for some disappointment. My father had once tried to interest me in great music by taking me with him to church in Aboyne. By way of demonstration he began to play the Bach G-minor Fugue, pedalling out its first entry with his feet. My reaction to this classic was immediate. The sight of my father, seated, performing a frantic dance with his lower limbs, sent me into fits of laughter, and it was some time before he allowed himself to see the funny side of it all.

In Edinburgh I was sent for piano lessons to a motherly soul who believed, I think, that since Father was already something of a celebrity his son should be cast in the same mould. She was soon disillusioned. My lack of ability at the keyboard was matched only by my disinclination to work. Father himself had neither the time nor the patience to guide my stumbling fingers through 'Fairy Tiptoes' and 'Happy Clouds'. On such occasions as I managed to commend those masterpieces to his attention he would ripple through the printed crochets and quavers like a dipper in a burn, and then proceed to extemporize on their thin themes until the massive Bechstein was reverberating like the sea. The effect was superb; but it left me feeling more frustrated and inept than ever. The shoemaker's bairns, they say, are aye the worst shod.

My keyboard misery ended one day on a visit to my grandparents in Dunfermline. From one of those incredible cupboards which harbour everything from spiders and encyclopedias to garden tools, they unearthed a half-size cello. Its aged strings were intact but its bridge was broken. A cigarette box was used as a *pro tem* support for the strings and I was allowed to saw out the most excruciating noises from its tortured frame. It gratified me enormously that Father's attempts to play it were at least as bad as mine and here was a heaven-sent opportunity to out-match him. The cello became my own instrument.

Piano lessons ceased from then on. I was sent to study the mystique of the cello under the severe blue eye of Miss Ruth Waddell who taught in rooms in Edinburgh's Castle Terrace. She too, I think, entertained the delusion that heredity and environment had chosen me for Great Things, and I was not slow to straighten her out. I showed no more than an average competence. Under my fingers Saint Saens' lovely and idyllic Swan never quite got out of first moult and remained a rather ugly duckling.

After a cello lesson one shining afternoon I made my way home along a path below the black and frowning brows of the castle rock. For some reason that infernal hill goat Randolph leaped into mind, bleating to me that scaling the cliff above was mere child's play. And like an idiot I believed him. I laid down my school books and somebody's Gavotte in G in a niche and began to climb.

A cleft in the rock offered easy ascent initially. Young saplings and tussocks of grass provided friendly hand-holds, but against the cold, moist cliff face progress became difficult. A small avalanche of stones began to scurry underfoot, and my heart seemed to flutter down with them. In a steeper cleft I had to press hands out sideways to lever myself upwards. The only sounds I remember were the chuckling of falling stones, and the thud of my pulse and the rasping of my breath. I wanted to go back, but I knew that I dare not; and at last I lay on my back on green sward under the castle wall, frightened but triumphant.

The view from the top was magnificent. The low hills of Fife rolled along the northern horizon beyond the Firth of Forth. I could see a wing of the Forth Bridge, the cranes of Granton and Leith. And all Edinburgh, tier upon tier, rose up towards me like some wedding cake iced by a coalman. Trains from the west and north tunnelled through the green gardens beneath like rigid worms. Directly below me the view deteriorated sickeningly: a small group of people gazed up at me, among them an ominous figure in uniform.

Any fear I had of making a descent was completely obliterated by the sight of my reception committee. To stay aloft any longer, I knew, would only make matters worse. I tried – and did not fail – to come down almost nonchalantly, as if climbing the central buttress of Edinburgh were part of my daily exercise. The policeman, I discovered, was a tolerant man, only recently recruited to such open-air committee work, and not altogether in sympathy with his chairman.

She was a battleship in woman's grey. Her armour plating ran stiffly from neck to lower calf without one single curve of female reassurance. She mounted a handbag to port and a rolled umbrella to starboard, and squawked through an aperture in her upper bridge. She had spied my maroon blazer far above her head and now was demanding revenge for her sense of outraged propriety.

'You're a wicked, wicked laddie,' she cried, shaking me by the shoulder. 'You could have got yourself killed climbing up there. It's boys like you who make trouble for other people, throwing stones at cats and stealing flowers. . . .'

I could not quite follow her train of thought, having neither a bouquet of cats nor flowers to show for my trouble. But I let her ramble on.

'And now,' she concluded triumphantly, 'the policeman is going to take your name and address – aren't you, constable? – and he'll report you to your father and headmaster, and that will mebbie teach you to behave.'

I looked apprehensively at the bobby and he, without batting an eyelid, contrived to wink at me. He heaved a sigh and produced a notebook and pencil.

'If you'll all just move along,' he said, 'I'll deal with the matter.' He made gentle shooing motions with his arms, and the battleship and her small, curious flotilla sailed reluctantly.

When they had gone he put his notebook and pencil away and looked at me solemnly.

'That was rather a silly ploy of yours,' he said. 'If you had got into trouble up there, I might have had a job getting you down. Always remember that when you go risking your neck you're also risking the necks of those who come to help you.'

I was suffused with a sense of shame. To think that I might have endangered this man's life and limb filled me with guilt. His stern but kindly lecture had more effect than any wigging, and I always remember his advice. He did ask my name and address – but that was simply so that he could walk me part of the way home.

Days in Edinburgh passed happily enough, but country longings burned in our blood. Father's weekly hours were spent in composing and arranging music and in building up the BBC Scottish Orchestra to symphonic standard. At weekends he had time to spare for country rambles.

We were lucky in having relatives in Roxburghshire. My Uncle George (my mother's brother in-law) had a joinery business at Manorhill, not far from Kelso. Even now I can smell the perfume, released by saw and chisel, of the fine wood in his long, cool shed. His garden, 100 miles more southerly than ours had been at Aboyne, was born of even greater plenty, and my Aunt Eliza's larder reflected its bounty: like my mother's other four sisters, she shared – and often excelled them – in the family art of finding a use for everything.

My cousin George – 'Young George', to distinguish him from his father – was eleven years older than I, and another hero of my tender years.

He was quiet as a boy, over-chattered perhaps by his two older sisters. When family tiffs threatened he would make for the woods and the river – the great brown-eyed Tweed which he loved so dearly.

He had learned to cup his hands and blow through his thumbs in imitation of a brown owl. And out of the Tweed-side woods one evening Jacob came, silent of wing and still with the great blue eyes of young owlhood, to perch miraculously on his shoulder in answer to his call. Conservationists might frown today, but Jacob came willingly to captivity. A strange *rapport* between boy and bird strengthened with the years: theirs was a love passing a great deal of understanding.

An aviary was built for Jacob complete with roosting box and perching tree. From his favourite branch he surveyed the world, displaying the ability of all owlkind to rotate his head through 180 degrees. Between Jacob and George's half-Persian cat a remarkable relationship developed, unguided by any human agency.

The cat spent much of her time hunting rats and mice in the stack-yard and outbuildings of a nearby farm. Although she did not eat her prey (she was too well fed for that) it seemed to cross her mind that here was provender going to waste; or perhaps the owl's interest in her field activities aroused the mother instinct in her. Whatever the reason, she acquired the habit of carrying her trophies to Jacob's cage. At her approach he would hunch his wings ready to swoop. Unflinchingly she would hold mouse or rat against the wire netting of his enclosure while Jacob's feathered talons hauled it inside. They had no beautiful pea-green boat, these two, but simply because it was real and natural their friendship seemed more marvellous than Lear's delightful fantasy.

More than once in his lifetime Jacob escaped from his cage. On each occasion young George went at dusk into the deep woods, sometimes spending the whole night hooting – sometimes bringing strange owls close to hand – and always feeling at last the softness of Jacob's feathers as he landed like a great moth on his shoulder.

My early ramblings with George along the Tweed filled me full, mind, body and soul. There was no birdsong that he did not recognize, no wild flower, no tree nor living creature. He had that gift, so rare among men, of dispelling fear among birds and animals. He once climbed a tree and brought down a clutch of five fledged starlings, sitting un-afraid in the cup of his hand. He showed me a blackbird's nest once, and while we fed small worms to the skinny youngsters, their mother came to perch on our fingers.

By the time I was eight or nine I had already made up my mind that whatever profession I chose it must be in some way connected with the lives of the lesser creatures.

I could not understand why human beings, with all their imperfections, were assured a place in heaven, while the rest of the animal kingdom, in all its delightful innocence, had seemingly to make do with consignment to oblivion.

Not long ago I read a newspaper report of a man who had cruelly tortured and murdered his baby son. The judge, pronouncing sentence on him, said: 'Your behaviour was little better than that of an animal.'

What a gross impeachment, surely, of the beasts of the field! Animals may kill, goodness knows, but name me one capable of coldly and ruthlessly planning and inflicting torture on its own young. Nature can be pretty raw, but it is at its rawest and ugliest in the darker areas of human society and I would rather have my tom-cat for company in eternity than some members of my own species.

I think it was my admiration for young George and his ways which inspired my first major literary effort. 'When I grow up,' I essayed laboriously, 'I would like to become an ornithologist.' It took me so long to get down 'ornithologist' correctly that posterity was denied the privilege of reading any more. Even at school in Edinburgh I seemed to have feathers on the brain. A diary was given to our class, each boy taking it in turn to record the interesting events of the day. When my own turn sadly coincided with the death of King George V, I was at pains to describe a violent squabble between starlings and sparrows in our garden, the state of the weather, and finally saw fit to mention that we had lost a beloved monarch. Mr MacDonald, our teacher, was not impressed.

'What an extraordinary sense of priorities Whyte has,' he informed the class, having read my diary contribution aloud.

Addressing me directly, he asked: 'Do you really think that people are more interested in sparrows and starlings than in the king's death. What do they feed you on at home – bird seed?'

My classmates squealed with delight and I allowed my scarlet face to reply for my stricken tongue. This, I think was my first lesson in journalism. It did nothing to curb my love of nature, but it helped me to see life in better perspective.

I got on pretty well with my contemporaries, especially with the boys who didn't fight. Girls became an increasing embarrassment to me. There was something intangibly desirable about them, but as nobody had bothered to tell me anything about sex, I was unable to define the strange feelings they aroused in me. The four-letter words I heard at school, I knew, had something to do with male-female relationships; but as these words were spoken in sniggering secrecy, and were obviously taboo, it seemed expedient to keep womankind at a safe distance.

The grown-ups in my young life were mostly relatives. My maternal grandparents lived in Edinburgh's Stockbridge, not far from our home. Grandpa McWhannell (a strange corruption of McDonald) was a thin blade of a man with a keen temper to match and a liking for neat whisky. Grannie was a sweet, plump soul with an accent which often puzzled me.

She pronounced 'car' as 'cawr' and 'far' as 'fawr'. Someone – probably my mother – must have tried to correct her at some time; for she also pronounced 'caught' as 'cat' and 'bought' as 'bat'. I vividly remember her struggling once to describe a small domestic drama.

'The caught cat a moose,' she said. 'No . . . the cat *catched* a moose . . . och, anyway – the wee beast's deid.'

Her invariable welcome to me was to fix her gaze at a point well above my head and murmur, 'My, what braw red cheeks you have!'

I could never fathom how she managed to study my complexion at this strange trajectory until I finally asked my mother about it.

'Granny's spectacles are bi-focal,' she explained.

Visits to my paternal grandparents in Dunfermline were fairly frequent. When I was eight or so I was allowed to make the train journey solo for the first time. Father saw me off at Waverley and as I raised my hand to wave proud farewell, he slammed shut the carriage door, imprisoning my right thumb. The train whistle and I shrieked simultaneously – and we were off. The door could not be opened from the inside, and the window had to be lowered before I could be freed. My thumb was the colour of a ripe damson and the pain the worst I had so far encountered.

Grandpa Whyte met me on arrival and soon cheered me up. All that would happen, he said, was that my nail would fall off and a bigger and better one grow in its place. He was dead right. Grandpa was one of the kindliest men I ever knew, a creature of infinite softness and patience, a man who, throughout his life, never sought beyond his modest station in life.

Every morning, when Hay and Robertsons' linen factory hooter blew, he would don his immaculate suit and put a fresh flower in his buttonhole. All day long he would sit at his desk, counting the profit and the loss, simultaneously adding four columns of figures; pounds, shillings, pence and halfpence. He was the perfect computer. He neither sought promotion nor asked for a rise. At a time when the linen trade was booming he cost his firm £5 per week. He gave them his lifetime, and when he retired they gave him a small present and a short speech of thanks – and wasn't he the proud man!

He believed in Socialism, however, and dreamed of a coming day when the dignity of work might earn greater reward.

Like most families, ours had a black sheep. My other Uncle George was enormously fat and jolly, the life and soul of any party. Ludicrously, he ran around, I remember, in a baby Austin whose driving seat barely accommodated his bulk, and whose springs squeaked like hurt mice whenever he rolled aboard.

When he laughed, which was often, he wobbled like a badly set jelly, setting up faint earth tremors and infecting everyone with his merriment. His favourite haunt was a pub – especially if there happened to be a piano handy. On a Friday or Saturday night his quips and funny stories attracted crowds of strangers. Moving to the piano, he would accompany his rich baritone through a repertoire of hilarious songs while drinks piled up before his grateful eyes. Gradually the mood of the music would change. Without realizing quite what was happening, plumbers, poulterers and window cleaners would find themselves singing Psalm 23 to the tune Crimond while tears of joy rolled down their cheeks.

Finally, when he knew that he held them captive, Uncle George would rise and deliver a sermon, brimful of angels and eternal love, while his congregation floated on a blissful sea of saintly brotherhood and unsanctified whisky. My Uncle George was a very religious man.

He had a succession of businesses in Edinburgh all of which seemed to collapse and my father on more than one occasion had to come to the rescue.

One summer in the thirties a visit of naval ships to Aberdeen coincided with the arrival of my uncle, gravely out of pocket. The sight of frigates in the bay provided the needed inspiration. With great heartiness he represented himself to the manager of a city bank as a rear-admiral. He had come ashore without his cheque book, he explained, and was in urgent need of £100. Aberdeen bank managers are not renowned for their gullibility, but Uncle George was no mean actor. He casually began name-dropping, quite shamelessly including dukes and earls among his acquaintances and the banker lapped it all up like a kitten.

Retribution followed, of course. But somehow my uncle was spared the worst. The matter was hushed up and all the ruffled feathers smoothed. Uncle George was the most lovable of men, and perhaps this quality was his saving grace. It was not long after this that he disappeared from the family circle.

Only a few years ago a religious pamphlet fluttered through my letterbox in Glasgow. It invited me to attend a church service at which the guest speaker would be a high dignitary of the church in America. I was about to throw the leaflet away when my eye was drawn to the portrait on the front. There, slightly greyer, slightly thinner and wearing his vestments of good office, was my reverend uncle. I could not resist winking at him.

Living in grey Edinburgh with its steep streets and grinding trams became fairly tolerable to me as a boy. Edinburgh men were hard and distant. Edinburgh women laced their minds as well as their bodies in vigorous corsets. I got used to the people, but never got to love them. I longed for the country and one day Father promised me a fishing holiday, back in Aberdeenshire among the hills of Glen Tanar. Oh, the stabbing joy of it! Even now I can feel the sweet pain of looking forward, the long ache of days which took months to crawl from dawn to dusk. But first of all I had to have my tonsils out.

I lay in a strange bed in Moray Place, shivering with fear. The ceiling above me, dimly lit, was midnight blue on which gilt stars were arrayed in dreadful symmetry. A nurse came to collect me at 7.30 a.m. and carried me up a long spiral staircase. The theatre doors opened silently and I entered a perfect chamber of horrors. My executioners stood robed in shrieking white, hooded and masked and wearing rubber gloves. Their table was already laid with scalpels, scissors, steaming trays, tweezers, forceps – all of shining silver. How lovingly they laid me on their clean tablecloth! How helplessly our family doctor smiled, and how soothingly the chief executioner said grace!

Gently ramming a huge block of rubber between my jaws, he murmured: 'There's a good boy. All I want you to do now is blow up this nice football.'

A ghastly red balloon floated above me. Four nurses had me pinned down, one at each corner. In desperation I decided to obey instructions and blow up the bladder. Ah, the cunning of the man! To blow something up you have first of all to inflate your lungs, and in doing so I inhaled the most nauseous vapour I had ever smelled, or have smelled since. Red stars and yellow lights flashed in my exploding brain as ether and air and God knows what else combined to send me into merciful oblivion.

My consequent sore throat was nothing compared to that pre-operative torture; but, alas, the days of premedication were not yet with us. Even the ice cream which had been faithfully promised me was not forthcoming.

But I don't think I really cared. Visions of foaming pools filled my mind, and the rattle of distant trams was drowned in the rush of imagined waterfalls. And through my head there ran the shapes of fish, silver and spotted, fresh from the sea and the Dee, breasting the stream to where it mingles with the clouds in the place that they and I both know as home.

4

The Writhing Heather

Father's expensive (£130 second-hand) Daimler, 1931
vintage, fairly pranced up the Devil's Elbow out of Perthshire and into my native county. I remember him singing
the praises of the modern engine and recalling the adventures
he had had there in the difficult days of motoring.

His first car had been a Calcott, and on his first ascent of
the then notorious double bend it had ground to a precarious
halt. The gradient was too steep even for first gear: he had
had to slither back down and turn the car on the narrow
road. Reverse gear, he had remembered, had a lower ratio
than first, and the climb was finally accomplished backwards.

Succeeding cars – a Galloway and a Bean – had managed
the ascent forwards. But at the top they had required rest,
like horses, and a long drink from a convenient well. Those
must have been pretty nerve-racking days. To be stuck on
the lonely Elbow on a winter's night with a blizzard imminent
was the dread, often realized, of many a motorist. I don't
think anyone ever perished there – at least not literally – but
Peter must have more than once had his hand ready to open
the gate upstairs.

The Daimler bellowed up in second gear, and her temperature gauge indicated that a stop for refreshment was quite
unnecessary. We were in high spirits; for there is nothing
worse in this world than a car that breaks down on its way
to the fishing. It may pack in on its way to work, to a wedding or to a Christmas party. It may even fold up on its way
home from the fishing if it feels so inclined. But the car which
fails to get you to the waterside is fit only for the scrapyard.

Once again the Dee, my mother river, ran in her valley wearing the blue and silver she borrows from the sky on decent days. The young brown Tanar ran to meet her, and our sandy road followed the stream up out of pine woods into open heather country fringed with mountains.

Our home for three weeks was Corrievrach, a small shooting lodge on the upper reaches of the Tanar Water. It had three rooms and boasted what in Scotland is called a 'shunkie' and elsewhere 'a primitive form of sanitation'. Our toilet resident was a large and lugubrious toad who was civil enough not to object to sharing his quarters with us when occasion demanded. A ventilator in the wall of the lodge was also occupied by a sleek and fat dormouse who spent much of his time sunbathing, waking up occasionally to scrub his white shirt front.

I couldn't wait to begin fishing. The water was low and my father led me upstream to where the Falls of Tanar tumbled into a deep pool. Clumsily I cast a worm into the dark eddies, watched the pink of it deepen to red and disappear in the peat water. And then – ah then! – there came that first electric, nibbling wriggle, the exquisite thrill of hooking the first trout – the four-ounce Leviathan – the only fish that ever mattered – that ever will matter, come to think of it. Scoring the first goal at football is nothing compared to this. Hitting the first long drive at golf, having your first article published, hearing the B Minor Mass for the first time, or the first mavis of spring, or even kissing a girl are all lesser sensations. Hooking that fish goes back to the burn of Eden. Adam knew all about it before he bothered with Eve, begat Cain and Abel, before he tasted apple.

There are always bigger fish to catch, but the first is always better. There is a Gaelic proverb which runs: 'The two most beautiful things in death – a dead child and a dead fish.' Perhaps only fishermen and poets are capable of understanding the truth of that.

The July sun blazed and I was happy – too happy I know now. One should always guard against being too happy. It simply makes sorrow all the worse.

There was I, tramping home triumphant through the ling in father's wake, when I trod on what my careless eyes took

44

to be a heather root. One end of it sprang up, as heather roots sometimes do. But heather roots neither hiss nor display long teeth.

I broke all records for the sideways standing leap, a performance which landed me on a boulder in the river. I stood there sobbing with terror, overcome with loathing. Father's questioning eyebrows were somewhere up among his hair. All I could do was point a quivering finger towards my place of take-off, and he investigated.

'It's an adder,' he muttered. 'It didn't bite you, did it?' I shook my head. My fear was not of being bitten. It was the appearance of the creature, the sinuous movement of it, which possessed me with horror. Father killed the poor thing with his boot, but even then I made my way homewards downstream, jumping from boulder to boulder. Nothing would induce me to walk through more heather.

Whether my plunge into the mill-dam at Aboyne had anything to do with it, or whether it stems from some primitive instinct, my horror of snakes, or anything resembling one, is almsot uncontrollable. All my life I have tried to make myself like them. I know that they are clean and dry-skinned, beautifully marked and relatively harmless. I know everything good there is to know about them. But even the sudden sight of one on TV or in an illustrated book is enough to make me leap in terror. If a wild leopard walked into the room I would at least go through the motions of making 'there's a good pussy-cat' noises. If the smallest grass snake came in at the door, I would go out via the window.

Glen Tanar that summer had a plague of adders – big black males with yellow zig-zags on their backs, and their less colourful brown mates. Sheep with dreadfully swollen limbs and lame deer bore testimony to their numbers. I stuck faithfully to the road, or to bare places where I could study the ground for yards around. But not even the adders could spoil my delight. By day the hill tops stayed aloof and distant. At dusk they seemed to gather in, and at night if you listened, as the eagle listens, you could hear the faint low roar of their breathing, the sound some people call silence. We walked a lot, covering up to twenty miles in a day. We climbed Mount Keen, that barren peak on the invisible border between the shires of Aberdeen and Angus, and gazed in rapture on the land unfolding around us. Distant villages shimmered under a blue haze, and thirty miles away was the vague blue-grey curve we knew to be the sea.

From a green pillow of sphagnum below the summit a spring bubbled. Putting my lips to it I sucked in cool sweet water – and a strange childish notion entered my head. If I drank enough, I imagined, I might arrest the Cowie Burn which rattled down the mountainside to join the Tanar. By depriving Tanar of a tributary I would diminish the mighty Dee, and even the sea beyond would shrink proportionately. I pictured myself, I think, as a kind of latter-day Canute, slyly influencing the tide by turning the tap off at source. My ignorance of the natural workings of rain-catchment could barely excuse such precocious conceit. And yet I fancy I had begun to see the glimmerings of the secret of life on earth, the eternal water cycle which quickens and sustains every living organism.

The cool cloud kisses the earth, lies with her and the spring is their issue. The young burn prattles in its cradle for a while, brawls into youth, leaping from ledge to ledge, and finally achieves the majority of riverhood. Ageing as it runs, the river acquires great dignity, begins to slow up and wander towards journey's end and sea oblivion. But there is no death there in the green cathedral deeps. The sun resurrects and once again the ardent clouds go wooing among the hills. Standing beside the bubbling well of a mountainside is perhaps as good a way as any to contemplate immortality.

The moss absorbs and the fly quivers. The tree grows and the trout darts. That tiny fountain at your feet flows through roots and foliage, through gills and bloodstreams. It helps to cool the feet of cattle, floats the swan and turns the slapping, dripping water wheel, makes milk and whisky, grinds corn and tempers steel, and sets the ships of all the world to sea. It catches every facet of the sun and every flicker of the moon and stars. It is completely colourless – and is still the embodiment of the rainbow.

How strange, therefore, that men should worship gold. But gold, you see, is rare and solid. It does not evaporate. It is malleable, as any smith or stockbroker will tell you, and can be bent to many uses. Blossom must contact blossom to propagate, and man must have his way with a maid, but gold begets gold by dint of an artificial reproductive system called usury. You can see this system at work in the banks of the world: only river banks maintain a natural and even growth.

It is gold which makes differences between man and man, and between them and their environment. It is water which creates all the similarities and familiarities, and I hope the day is coming when that most precious of all elements will be accorded its true value.

The power and the magic of water seemed marvellous to me even as a child, and during that hot summer my father determined to put it to good use.

Far down the Tanar in its deepest pools salmon and sea-trout lay poised like arrows. Only a spate could supply them the energy and assurance to launch themselves upstream into the thinner waters of Corrievrach. If we built a dam, Father argued, we could create quite a deep pool. And if we suddenly breached it, the ensuing flood might encourage the fish to run. The sheer majesty of the idea enthralled me. Our hydro scheme began in earnest.

Father chose a pool with a plentiful supply of building material, rolling heavy boulders into position. My job was to fill in the gaps and cracks with lesser stones and gravel. A stick cut with notches acted as a water mark, and we were gratified to see the level rising, inch by precious inch. Each time a boulder was moved the stream would change course, threatening the weaker parts of our dam and each time I splashed to their defence. As the water deepened so did its voice, changing almost imperceptibly from soprano to alto; and as our pool deepened it also increased in breadth, forcing us to extend our rampart on either side. A bulldozer would have shortened our labours but, on reflection, it would have spoiled our fun by half.

When our dam was three or four feet high, Father called a halt. We would now wait until nightfall to perform the opening ceremony, he decreed, his reason being that seatrout prefer travelling in the dark. The centre part of our dam was part of an old door, and this he proposed to raise, allowing the pent up water to escape. He wobbled out to it like a nervous tight-rope walker, seized it and hauled it up. And the ensuing moments were in the finest slapstick tradition. An enormous gout of water surged through the gap with a leonine roar. In a vain endeavour to retain his balance Father jettisoned the door and fell backwards into what was left of our pool. The door, borne on the crest of the flood, went spinning downstream, and I collapsed in hysterics of laughter. The rumblings of our deluge faded fairly rapidly and peace returned to the glen.

What the fish though of a flood-happy door thundering through their domain will never be recorded. I spent a sleepless hour or two in bed that night, listening for their arrival. Vague whispers and gurgles from the dark river set my limbs trembling with delicious electricity, and I fell asleep with a three-pounder tucked somewhere safely between my pillow and my dreams.

I was up like a flushed snipe at daybreak, zig-zagging over adderless ground to our pool. In the clear dawn water of youth and truth I could see little fish darting – young trout and salmon parr with the mauve imprints of St Peter's fingers dabbed on their innocent ecumenical skins. But not a single seatrout was in residence. I knew that for a fact, for I ventured an exploring hand round every stone and shelf of rock. After all, I remembered retrospectively, our home-brewed spate had been rather a puny effort, dissipating its force within a few hundred yards of origin. What seatrout, feeling the million-millionth fraction of its force, would quicken fins in prospect of a honeymoon?

I ate a dispirited breakfast and half-heartedly followed my father down the sandy road. He stopped opposite the pool into which the Cowie Burn drops like a staircase of brown lino flats and creamy falls. Between ourselves and the pool lay fifty yards of dreaded writhing heather. I stood my ground and he read my thoughts.

He grasped my hand and crashed through the heather tangle. Any snake in our path must have high-tailed it for the nearest hole. I certainly didn't see any, but perhaps that's because my eyes were tightly shut.

The Cowie Burn joined the Tanar in a final fine cascade. With a flick of his little seven-foot cane rod, Father dropped a small red worm into the froth below the fall, and let it dribble around with the current. As his line drifted into the mainstream it halted momentarily. Crouched like a cat, he raised his rod point. When it quivered he struck. The reel shrieked. But many decibels above that screech of metal came the sound of his voice shouting: 'SEATROUT! . . .' and the corries of Mount Keen yelled back: 'Seatrout . . . out, out . . . tea's out . . . sauerkraut. . . .'

From the confluence of waters a perfect half moon of a fish rose and set several times within seconds. It might have confined its gymnastics to the river pool, but for some odd reason decided to take to the staircase of the Cowie Burn, leaping fall after fall with the grace and power of an Olympic hurdler. Father watched his line disappearing up the hillside and elected to give chase. He surged waist deep through the Tanar, emerged at a squelching gallop on the farther bank and began to pursue his fish up-burn. A small cliff presented itself as an obstacle to man – but not to beast. The seatrout leaped through a fissure too narrow to admit its pursuer and sounded in the pool above. I watched my father recklessly throwing his rod to the ledge overhead, hauling himself up and resuming the battle. He was bending down to grab the fish by the gills when it acquired a new lease of power and hurtled headlong back into the Tanar. My parent did not quail. He followed like a mountain goat, springing from ledge to ledge. His final jump landed him in the pool where he had first hooked his quarry, and there the battle ended with the two contestants evenly wet.

That splendid silver fish weighed nearly four pounds. My father cut a stem of bracken and threaded it through gills and mouth to serve as a handle. I tried to count the black spots on that trout as we trudged home, but walking made them jiggle up and down and the sunlight on its scales dazzled my eyes.

I asked my father if he thought our mini-spate had enticed that fish upstream. He thought it possible; for were not fish the most wonderfully sensitive of creatures? The fall of a shadow or footstep is enough to send them darting for cover.

49

The least rise or drop in temperature or barometric pressure, imperceptible to us, is sufficient to affect their behaviour. Why then should not our artifice have subtly governed events?

Collecting provisions from Aboyne entailed a round journey of twenty miles and the waste of half a day – until Mr Strachan, the grocer in Station Square, hit on a novel idea.

'Take this hamper of carrier pigeons,' he offered. 'Wrap your order round a doo's foot and fly it down to me. Our van goes up the length of Etnach, and you'll only have two miles to travel for your groceries.'

We took the birds – twelve soft crooning creatures with round eyes and pink feet – and installed their hamper in an outhouse. It became my job to feed and water them, Father having a loathing of feathers which eclipsed even my horror of snakes. On my first catering mission I discovered that one of our ladies had laid an egg in the hamper – but which bird was Mum? It seemed grossly unfair to pick an expectant mother out of confinement, garter her pretty leg with an order for sugar, tea and bacon and bid her fly this intelligence to Aboyne. I decided to keep close watch. Whichever pigeon elected to sit on the egg, I argued, must prove to be the owner, and, having identified her, we could then dispatch any one of the remaining eleven as messenger. But I had a lot to learn about pigeon perversity.

All twelve looked alike. If I stayed quiet everyone wanted a shot at incubation, jostling for position. If I moved a muscle everyone shuffled away, disowning the egg as if it had been a poison capsule. And what kind of trade unionism was this?

I decided to give the egg the maternal benefit of our oven until such time as we could return it to Mr Strachan. Mercifully perhaps we were spared the pains of rearing a baby pigeon, for the egg proved to be infertile.

When it came time to send an order, we chose the smallest and thinnest piece of paper we could find, and utilized Father's ability to write legibly as well as microscopically; for we couldn't very well bandage our messenger's leg with a sheet of notepaper, however well folded. We chose the strongest looking bird, and I was allowed to perform the launching ceremony. Our postman rose with a fine clatter of wings, circled the house thrice and abruptly landed on the roof. A severe itch in his trousers was apparently a matter requiring urgent attention, and he sat there preening and fluffing for fully ten minutes. The effort seemed to exhaust him for he shortly fell asleep. My father began shelling him (it could have been her, mind you) with small bore chips of gravel, but this had no effect. To use larger ammunition would have been risky: there is a subtle distinction to be drawn between activating one's errand boy and annihilating him completely. We held a family conference.

My offer to climb the roof was flatly rejected, two to one. So too was father's suggestion that we forget the groceries and eat the pigeons. My objection to that idea was purely sentimental. Mother's was more logical.

'If you want roast pigeon,' she counselled, 'you'll have to do without vegetables. If you want vegetables, you'll have to send pigeons.'

Father got the point – and I wasn't slow in crashing in with another brilliant idea. 'Let's write the message out again and send another pigeon,' I said. Mother shook her head. 'If we do that,' she said, 'the first pigeon might follow the second, and that would mean two orders being delivered.'

When darkness fell, the bird on the roof was still roosting. By morning he had gone, but never reached his destination. Perhaps some peregrine culled him from the skies, or perhaps he teamed up with wild kindred. Whatever his fate, our provisions did not arrive. When three more pigeons failed to reach Aboyne, we returned the remainder to Mr Strachan. Pigeons, I decided, were charming creatures: telephones might be handier but not so lovable, and not quite so unpredictable. I learned at first hand how Noah must have felt when he released his dove. Unlike Noah, I had not the joy of discovering from a bird that the world's grocery store was still open for business.

The loss of those creatures saddened me. When the wind blew down a telephone wire you did not think about ruptured metal. You rattled the telephone rest and yelled for an operator. But when a pigeon went astray you worried about a light bundle of flesh, blood and feathers. And suddenly you found yourself asking in more civil tones for the operator, and wondering how, across the gulf between time and eternity, you might communicate. And this, I suppose, is what is called prayer, although I learned to mistrust the word.

When the dreich organ of my childhood wheezed under the cold fingers of some thin old maid, and when a cough in church barked the shins of God, I could not pray. When the pew creaked and the crimson velvet bag was passed around by a man in shiny pin-striped trousers and a shiny pin-striped mind, I could not pray. I paid up in silence. When the minister rose to his pulpit like a wingless rook, I lowered my eyes in deference to the Almighty fact that the Women's Guild would meet on Wednesday.

Sometimes, when a shaft of sunlight arrowed through stained glass, or when jackdaws chuckled in graveyard trees, I became aware of God's necessary laughter and the guilty feeling that He might be praying for me. Sometimes a happy choice of phrase from the minister's lips would shatter the monotony of his reverend delivery into a sparkle of truth – like a pebble thrown into a black pond.

I began to suspect that God was much too impersonally great to be involved in the petty squabbles of His interpreters. Only in the calm contemplation of the stars, in the discipline of living tolerance, in the ordered mysticism of great art and greater humility, in the melting pot of pure wonderment, could one begin to glimpse the author of all creation. The trouble is that we have reconstructed God in our own image, appointing Him chairman and giving Him a bank balance while we get on with the mundane task of ruining His business.

Theology and religion did not oppress my younger days. Neither of my parents was an ardent church-goer, although my mother occasionally prophesied hell-fire and damnation as punishment for our non-attendance.

Religion for me, even when young, was nearly synonymous with nature. To stand under the blue canopy of day or the black bridge of night was to be in church, and every day was a day of worship. Thunderstorm, earthquake and hurricane were the tools of creation. To see the result of their architecture I had only to look towards the mountains.

Great scenery, I learned to think, is simply great architecture: one drinks it in enormous gulps, and so filled does one become that one is forced to pour back something of oneself – to recreate in the original meaning of the word. Recreation is perhaps best understood by farmers and artists, least well by those who take everything their environment has to offer and give little or nothing in return.

Three weeks at Corrievrach were enough to convince me that whatever I did with my life, it must be connected, however tangentially, with the countryside and its creatures.

The freedom of the glen came to an end. Once again the grey hive of the city buzzed dismal welcome. But the strings of memory are mercifully strong. If I tried hard enough to shut out all distractions, the Tanar rippled down Lothian Road and seatrout ran for Tollcross and Braid Hills beyond.

5

Piano-tuners and Poachers

The doorbell of our Edinburgh home rang one afternoon when my mother was expecting the arrival of a piano-tuner. On opening the door she was confronted by a small man with Latin features, rather shabbily dressed and out of breath.

'Ah, you've come about the piano,' she said sweetly. 'Will you be terribly long? – I have to go out this afternoon.'

'I shall be about two hours,' said the little man, 'but please go out if you wish. If you would kindly show me where the piano is. . . .'

Two hours seemed to Mother an excessive time in which to tune a well-kept Bechstein. Neither did she relish leaving an unknown tradesman loose in the house. Her manner stiffened a little.

'The piano is in here,' she said. 'But please be as quick as you can. I shall wait until you are finished.'

Fuming inwardly, she closed the drawing-room door on him – and was almost immediately amazed to hear enormous cascades of Beethoven flooding the house. Annoyance gave way to delight, but reasserted itself when, after an hour, there was no audible sign of any tuning being done. Thinking that a cup of tea might expedite matters, she took one in to her musical artisan. She was rather shocked when, scarcely pausing between chords, he brusquely swept her offering aside.

'Thank you,' he said, 'but I am too busy. I am working against time.' His playing continued *maestoso*. Mother swept out *con brio*. A further hour later the music ceased and its exponent left the house *prestissimo*. How I wish I had been a fly on the wall that afternoon!

When Father arrived home in the evening, he asked casually: 'John arrived, I suppose? I'm sorry I hadn't time to phone you that he was coming.'

'He arrived,' my mother said acidly. 'And a more discourteous man I have seldom met.'

She informed my father that, while it might be amusing to be treated to an afternoon's piano recital, and however gifted the pianist might be, it was nevertheless the duty of a tuner to be heard to be tuning, and not to spurn offers of tea, and never to leave the premises without at least saying goodbye; and who was this 'John' anyway who seemed to use our piano as a training field for his thwarted talent?

The tears of laughter coursing down my father's cheeks served only to worsen her perplexity. 'Who *was* that man?' she demanded.

'John Barbirolli,' my father managed to gasp. 'He needed somewhere to study before conducting tonight. I sent him down here.'

Poor Mother was horrified. She was the kind of person who, by dint of her upbringing, could bring poise and grace to any formal occasion. Prepared, she was the perfect hostess. Unprepared for informality, she shot like a hermit crab into a hard shell of self-protection. Many people in her lifetime mistook the shell and the vaguely waving pincers for the real soft person inside. She was chronically shy – an impediment I inherited from her; but instead of allowing herself and other people to relax, she would retreat into the exoskeleton of etiquette. She exuded snobbery, but was, in fact, one of the least snobbish people I have known. She lacked the ready wit necessary to fence with friends and repulse strangers. Extemporization was not one of her gifts. There were people she liked and those she did not. Company pleased her only momentarily: for Mother there seemed some inner virtue in loneliness.

Not many months before his death I had occasion to interview Sir John Barbirolli on his last visit to Glasgow to conduct the Scottish National Orchestra. I asked him about his encounter with Mother. Did he remember being mistaken for a piano-tuner?

His brown eyes twinkled. 'My roles increase,' he laughed.

'I have been ice-cream merchant and *haute couturier* in my time, but never before piano-tuner. How I wish I were so gifted!'

He remembered his visit to our house – but retained the vague impression that Mother had been the housekeeper!

Good fun and good music were almost inseparable when Father was around. He was gifted with an incredibly acute and accurate ear – a kind of Jodrell Bank scanner which could detect one wrong note amid the mass noise of seventy orchestral players – which made him a stickler for perfection, almost to a fault. When he felt that his aural powers required some intensive training he would get me to play a random fistful of notes on the piano. No matter how cacophonous the chord, he would unerringly name each component note. Not even domestic appliances were immune from his critical lug. Our vacuum cleaner was in G and the pantry door squeaked C sharp. In a friend's house one evening he astounded guests by complaining that the bathroom plumbing sounded a very flat D and was badly in need of tuning.

Members of the BBC Scottish Ochestra lived in some awe of his tongue as well as his ear. His bass section sat gawking during a rehearsal when he told them: 'Gentlemen, you are making a noise like a herd of pregnant elephants.'

On yet another occasion a lady fiddler (he hated the word 'violinist') verged on hysteria when told she sounded like a bum-bee's waistcoat.

Only once do I remember the biter bitten. Having just auditioned a talented young singer, he praised her vocal ability but suggested that she pay a little more attention to her vowels.

Some days later he received a letter. 'Dear Mr Whyte, thank you for auditioning me the other day. I have since seen my doctor and he tells me that there is nothing at all wrong with my bowels. . . .'

One of Edinburgh's majestic musical figures in my early days was Sir Donald Tovey, a man of immense scholarship perhaps best remembered today for his editing of Bach's Forty-Eight Preludes and Fugues. Like the legendary professor, Sir Donald tended sometimes towards absentmindedness, and Father took advantage of this to play rather a mischievous trick on him.

Tovey was due to rehearse Herold's overture Zampa with Edinburgh's Reid Orchestra when Father gathered a cluster of the players around him. Zampa begins 'tiddley-die pom pom, tiddley-die pom pom' – four beats to the bar. Father's instruction to the musicians was to add an extra 'pom' at the end of each of the first two bars.

'Tiddley-die pom pom pom' sounds neither unmusical nor ungrammatic – but it has the effect of converting four-four time into five-four. In all innocence Sir Donald mounted the rostrum, asked for Zampa, tapped the stand with his stick, and the fun began. Instead of ending the first bar on an up-beat, the unhappy conductor found himself making the down-beat of the next bar. By the beginning of the third bar he was clawing the air like a lion demented.

Scanning the score anxiously, he reassured himself that there were in fact four beats to the bar and started all over again. To a man the orchestra responded with 'Tiddley-die pom pom pom' while Sir Donald seemed to be knitting some involved and invisible pullover. Fine musician as he was, he could not for the life of him discover what was wrong, and suppressed orchestral mirth did nothing to ease his burden or resolve his problem. Eventually Father had to own up to his trick, and Sir Donald joined Queen Victoria and our former neighbour Miss Jamieson in being not exactly amused.

The term 'serious music' was frowned on by my father. 'There is only good music and bad music,' he used to say. 'Some good music – funeral marches and such – might be termed serious. But all bad music is extremely serious.'

Father's lined and forbidding face suggested that he had been sculptured rather than born, but laughter followed him faithfully. His idol was Arturo Toscanini, the little Italian maestro under whose baton Beethoven seemed to draw fresh breath. Father was fortunate to be in London when Toscanini was guest conductor with the BBC Symphony Orchestra, and attended a rehearsal in the Queen's Hall. The maestro, who could sniff out a missing dot in a symphony-load of crotchets, was not noted for evenness of temper.

On this occasion Toscanini was wearing a light alpaca jacket with a large handkerchief (he had a cold) stuffed up one sleeve. Each down-beat he made served to send the hankie flapping around his wrist. Every so often he would bring the orchestra to a halt and angrily ram the offending clout back up his sleeve. Having stopped rehearsal for the umpteenth time, he finally seized the handkerchief in passionate frenzy and hurled it behind him

Sir Adrian Boult, the orchestra's regular conductor and the mildest of men, elected to come in at that moment to see how everything was going. The first thing he saw was Toscanini's hankie floating to the floor. He walked forward. He picked it up. He interrupted rehearsal for the umpteenth time.

'Excuse me, signor,' he said with imponderable English calm, 'I think you have dropped your handkerchief.'

In the ensuing furore Father crept out, thankful that for once he had not been the instigator of another innocent crime.

The making of music was fun for those who were good at making it. For me, grinding painfully into the thumb position on my three-quarter sized cello, it was something of a chore. If I showed any flair at all in my callow years, it lay in drawing, painting and writing. I had a passion for painting lonely landscapes in which a small house nestled in the shelter of Scots pines. A river, brimful of fish of course, ran convenient to the door. Freud might have made much of such escapist art.

My literary heroes were people like H. Mortimer Batten, Seton Gordon, Jack London and Zane Grey. Any tale concerning animals or birds commanded my unswerving attention. As a result my school compositions fairly bristled with fur, hair and feathers. The human race seemed hardly worthy of mention.

On holiday at Dunkeld when I was ten, I made friends with a superb yellow Labrador called Snipe, a dog whose reasoning powers were above average. He had it worked out that if he pinched my school-cap and dangled it in front of me, just out of reach, I would be bound to follow him to reclaim my property. With the grace of a bull-fighter he would avoid my rushes and lead me inexorably towards the golfcourse – not merely to the course in general but to the fourth hole in particular.

Having lured me there, I suppose to stand guarantor for him, Snipe would drop my cap at my feet and plunge into an adjoining wood. Within minutes he would reappear with a hedgehog, gingerly carrying it by its prickle tips. Having laid one urchin at my feet, he would go back for another. Had hedgehogs been in the giant panda class of merchandise I might have become a millionaire.

Ignoring his spiky gifts and setting off homewards did nothing to curb his enthusiasm. Those damned balls of torture had to come along too. By the end of my holiday he had presented me with seven. His method of transporting them was ingenious. He would carefully carry one to the top of a hillock, bark, and send the creature rolling downhill, impaling leaves and grasses as it went. Thus cushioning its spikes, Snipe bowled his prize along Dunkeld's main street with a forepaw, bringing motorists to a squealing halt at the sight of a dog apparently playing football.

Snipe belonged to Mr and Mrs David Wilson of the Royal Hotel – royal, I suppose, because the inevitable Queen Victoria had once slept there. Her room was occupied by a large, lugubrious and elderly bachelor who seemed to frown on small boys, strong drink, dogs and late hours – on anything, in fact, which afforded pleasure to most holidaymakers.

Snipe's hedgehogs inspired us with the most appalling notion: we would put one of them in Mr Stronach's bed. The dire deed was performed shortly before his 10 p.m. retiral. It was one of these spur-of-the-moment acts which, no sooner done could not be undone. All the hotel guests were in on it; but even the safety of numbers could not allay the ghost of panic which chilled our backbones.

Mr Stronach retired. As was his custom he wished none a good night. The door of Queen Victoria's bedroom closed behind him. We sat in electric silence trying not to giggle. No sound came from the room above. Someone said: 'Hedgehogs are full of fleas, you know' – adding a new dimension to our outrage. Minutes crawled past like cold snails on a wall. Had the hedgehog gone to sleep outwith the reach of Mr Stronach's tender feet? Had the fleas adhered to their original host? Was it too late to visit his room, confess our guilt and hope for forgiveness?

And suddenly at the top of the stairs there stood an apparition clad in a voluminous nightgown. In one hand he held a face towel, in the other a pair of fire tongs. On top of the towel our hedgehog lay curled. For a full minute Mr Stronach did not speak. He stared at us and we stared back. The loudest noise in the lounge was the hammering of hearts. And then he spoke.

'Queen Victoria,' he announced, 'has left her false teeth in my bed.' We shrieked with the blessed relief of laughter, and Mr Stronach permitted himself the first wisp of a smile. 'I think,' he said, 'I shall come down and join you in a nightcap.'

Mr Stronach was applauded into our midst and backslapped until his shoulders must have ached. He was, it turned out, an immensely shy man requiring just such a prank to draw him from his shell.

Snipe's hedgehogs were released in a nearby garden save for two youngsters which I was allowed to take home with me to Edinburgh.

Peter and Joey settled happily in our city shrubbery, living on worms and slugs and coming out each evening when called for a supplementary diet of bread and milk. They further added grist to my mill by providing a subject for composition. Mr MacDonald, my English teacher, must have watched my skin for signs of incipient spikes.

But one man gave me encouragement. One day my father brought a burly, bespectacled giant home with him. Music was one of his loves, but surpassing it by far was his worship of the wild and his prowess in writing about rural Scotland. Ian MacPherson owed his ancestry, I think, to Badenoch, but his accent was nurtured somewhere between Inverness and Aberdeen in that corner of the land where the loveliest and most articulate English is still exclusively spoken. From his lilting tongue the eagle sailed and the peregrine took wing.

He was a passionate but never passive Highlander.

Absentee landlords were his *bêtes-noires*. Even those who held estate tenure the year round represented a breed of usurpers worthy of critical scrutiny. Much as the bitterness of the dole queue lingers in the blood of a Clydesider, so the outrage of the Highland Clearances was acid in his arteries. 'A stag from the hill, a fish from the river and a stick from the wood are the right of every man' he was fond of quoting from the Gaelic proverb. He was capable too, I was to discover, of practising what he preached.

'Come and stay in my cottage next summer,' he invited Father. 'You can have it to yourselves for a month. There are lochs for fishing and a burn at the door. The nearest neighbours are three miles away.'

How my heart sang when my parents accepted Ian's offer – but how slowly the months dragged their way towards promised days in a promised land.

The cottage lay half-way between Dalwhinnie and Laggan Bridge, a whitewashed sanctuary on a tract of rolling brown moorland. Ian and his wife were living in a caravan nearby when we arrived. Somehow I knew that adventure lay in wait.

In bed that first night I could not sleep: an incessant scurry of small animals put paid to that, pattering between walls and roof, bent on some pressing business or other. Around midnight there came the sound of a car and a knock at the door. Father's hastily lit oil lantern revealed Ian on the threshold. A small hind was slung across his shoulders.

'I've brought your breakfast,' he grinned. 'Come into the shed and help me with the gralloch.'

Our host, it transpired, had been returning from Dalwhinnie. His car headlights had reflected the red eyes of a deer. While the car was still moving he had opened the door, seized his rifle and shot her cleanly through the neck. Such marksmanship verged on the miraculous.

Mother was less excited by the deer than by the livestock in the walls. 'I think you've got rats in the house,' she told Ian.

He was horrified. 'Those aren't rats you're hearing,' he snorted – 'they're weasels. They drove the rats out years ago.'

We dined on deer's liver next day, and never a weasel

61

showed snout on that or any other day although the scurrying continued nightly. My mother had some misgivings about having weasels as lodgers and a poacher as a landlord, but Father and I were enthralled. Adventure was beckoning; real living was in crescendo.

On a shining day when the wind was shepherding wool in a high blue field, Ian took us on safari to Loch Laggan, in those days famed for fine fighting trout as richly coloured and dappled as any in the country. He baited a night-line with a bunch of worms and unashamedly hurled this illicit device into the loch at the mouth of a burn.

When we returned to it an hour or so later two fly fishers were drifting inshore towards us, directly above our line. Ian squatted pretending to be washing his hands but in reality coiling line at his feet.

'There's a fish on – a big one,' he whispered. And like an echo, a voice from the boat yelled, 'I'm into a fish! It's a good one I think.'

Ian swore under his breath. 'That fellow has hooked our line,' he muttered. 'It's our fish he's playing.'

The boat was less than thirty yards distant and drifting closer. Pretending to swat a cleg on his ear, Ian gave the line a savage jerk, sufficient to break the unfortunate angler's cast, but not enough to lose the trout. But now another crisis was looming.

My father hissed: 'There's a fisherman walking down the burn behind us – for heaven's sake watch what you're doing!'

Incredibly and with scarcely a ripple Ian guided our fish into the shallows. A dorsal fin and a tail as broad as a child's spade showed above the surface. The men in the boat were too busy lamenting their loss to notice, but the man behind us was now only ten yards away. A final heave fetched our trout ashore – all $4\frac{3}{4}$ pounds of him. Within seconds the hook was out, the fish dispatched and lowered inside the leg of Ian's trousers.

Standing up and being careful to conceal the line with his feet, Ian swung round in time to greet the man behind him.

'Hello,' he said cordially, 'are you having much luck with the fish?' The other grimaced. 'One or two small ones – but those fellows in the boat seem to have lost a beauty.'

'I noticed that,' Ian said blandly. 'Still, one can't be lucky all of the time.'

Father held me tightly by the hand. I could feel his unspoken message quivering up my arm: 'If you as much as open your mouth I'll skin you alive.' But I was beyond speech, utterly lost in admiration of the coolest nerve I ever met.

The following day I was asked if I knew what was meant by the word tact.

'I think so,' I said. 'It means not saying something stupid in front of other people.'

'That's not bad,' Ian said. 'Your dad and you are coming with me to see a gamekeeper, and whatever you do I want you to be tactful.' His eyes sparkled behind bottle-glass lenses. 'We've got a real adventure in mind.'

The gamekeeper, I remember, was a shrewd, suspicious character, very much his master's man. Ian MacPherson's reputation for seasonal exploits had apparently marched ahead of him. But under his persuasive tongue the keeper began to thaw visibly.

'I'm not against a bit of poaching myself, as you probably know,' Ian was saying. 'But when it comes to commercial poaching on a big scale I think it's time to draw the line – I think you'll agree.'

He went on to say that he had wind of a gang of poachers planning to raid one of the estate lochs the next day, and could he and his friend Ian Whyte 'of the BBC' be of any help in foiling the attempt?

So convincing was this discourse that the gamekeeper swallowed the lot. He was most grateful for this information, he said. He and his fellow keepers would keep close watch and, no thanks – outside help would not be needed. The meeting ended in great cordiality. On our way home to the cottage Ian explained the purpose of our mission. While all the estate keepers were patiently awaiting fictitious poachers, we would be several miles away – poaching the loch of Bhealaich Bheithe on the shoulder of Ben Alder.

I was sent to bed early that night and somehow managed to sleep despite tingling nerves and bustling weasels. Father wakened me at 4.30 a.m. The weather had broken and a storm was brewing.

In the thin grey light of summer dawn I shivered like the moorland grasses. The wind seemed to ripple my bloodstream and I was too young to feel any apprehension or guilt.

At 5 a.m. we drove to Dalwhinnie. Beside a boat belonging to the still soundly sleeping Loch Ericht Hotel, two other conspirators, friends of Ian, were skulking with a 'borrowed' outboard engine. We all set off into a snarling sou'westerly, bound for a bay beside Prince Charlie's cave nine miles down the white-capped loch. July was the month, but it had begun to snow. Above the grey veils of Ben Alder lightning flashed and thunder clattered.

And now a three-mile trek up a hill pathway lay ahead. Water cascaded down every step and stair of it. It became more comfortable to have my feet wet and warm than relatively dry and cold. Father, I think, was suffering agonies of remorse at allowing me to go on this expedition; but there was no turning back and he wisely kept silent. At last the dark shape of a boathouse loomed through the mist, and never was refuge more welcome. My elders managed to light a heather fire in the doorway and not even choking smoke could spoil the pleasure of its warmth. Father stripped me to the skin and for the first time in my life I was given a tot of whisky: the taste was vile, but the effect was warming – and made me feel no end of a man.

Ian and his two friends had put the rods up and gone to fish Bhealaich from the shore: they were back within ten minutes with a dozen fish, some of them topping the one-pound mark. I could barely wait for the boat to be launched and take my perch in the bows. Catspaws – tiger-swipes better describes them – scoured the loch. For a full and amazing minute a whirling column of water rose to join its counterpart descending from the low clouds overhead.

'Waterspout!' cried Ian at the oars, adroitly swerving the boat. The column glanced across our transom, blinding us with spray and spinning us in a circle. At a height of 3000 feet above sea-level a storm on a mountain loch is something to remember – and respect.

Butcher, Peter Ross, Greenwell, or whatever fly we pleased, had only to brush the waves to be snatched by wild rapacious trout. Thunder, snow, wind and hail could not dull their appetite. Father landed three at once on the same cast. Even when my own Devon minnow was still airborne there were fish snapping at its flying trebles. Such was the weather that we stuck it out for less than two hours, but in that time nearly sixty fish went into the bag.

The long journey home was wearisome indeed, but the sagging weight of trout on my companions' backs (companions, the child said) seemed to lighten by the hour. Any sense of guilt my father and I may have had was remedied by Ian's jolting comments on the streaming pathway homewards.

'You can hardly fish a loch like that to death . . . a catch like ours today leaves room for bigger fish to grow . . . and think of breakfast-time tomorrow . . . old folk with trout in the pan.

'Trout fishing should be like farming . . . enough to grace people's tables without ruining the field . . . no man has the right to anything he cannot utilize . . . no man has the right to take wild life for sport alone . . . the waste of living things is deplorable. . . .'

The sun came out and glistened on the scales sticking to his hands. The wetness of a pale blue shirt clung to his chest, and his words clung like limpets to my listening ears.

To Ian the Glorious Twelfth was a bird massacre perpetrated by an unfeeling aristocracy. His glory came on the eleventh when, at first light, he would slip past the watchful eyes of gamekeepers and cull a couple of brace of grouse from each of the surrounding moors. He was Buchan's 'John McNab' incarnate. When he was killed in a road accident Scotland lost a great, if rebellious, sportsman – and a small boy lost another of his heroes.

It was he who taught me field craft, to walk quietly as the cat walks, to read the weather story etched by wind on the loch or printed by clouds on the mountains. I determined to acquire his fine physique, his keen eye and ear, and above all his ability to make living a splendid adventure.

I did not know then that adventure of a kind undreamed of was lying in wait for me just below the shimmering horizon.

6

Down – and Up Again

My head ached, my legs felt like lead, and the leaden golf
ball I was sclaffing on Duddingston Golf Course trundled
from rough to rough.

Uncle Bert, my father's younger brother, looked at me in
some surprise. Already that morning I had gone round the
Braid Hills course in eighty-eight, which I think was not
disgraceful for a twelve-year-old. And now the delight of
hitting crisp shots had gone. At the half-way mark I stood at
something over level sevens.

My uncle, a fine all-round athlete, tried cajolery. 'Come
on,' he teased. 'You're playing like an old horse. You can do
much better than that.'

Normally his words would have spryed me up and put
some smeddum into me, but to my intense shame I found
myself blinking back tears.

'I'm terribly thirsty,' I mumbled, and Bert (as I always
called him) bought me a bottle of limeade from a kiosk
nearby. The bright green liquid somewhat assuaged my
thirst but turned my knees to jelly. The last thing I wanted
was to spoil Bert's game. I tried to go on but could not.
Recollections of our journey home and the events of the next
fortnight are vague and sporadic. The date was 3 September
1938. Exactly a year before the outbreak of war I was starting
a private conflict of my own.

I remember Mother taking my temperature and sending
me to bed . . . calling vainly for her when my nose began to
gush blood, crimsoning the bed sheets . . . thinking, in
delirium, that I was a pike and trying to wrench a hook from

my mouth . . . swimming feebly in a vast sea of pain that
seemed to fill my known world . . . seeing the disembodied
face of Dr Morris, our GP, and hearing him saying something about influenza . . .

What I do not remember were the murmured consult-
ations of specialists, the final diagnosis, the urgent SOS for
an iron lung, and the discovery that the nearest one was in
Leeds – and in use.

Nor do I remember how my father, for eight interminable
hours, kept me alive by raising and lowering my chest, four
beats to the bar, seventy crotchets to the minute, until he
himself was half dead with exhaustion. Happy the father
who begets his son twice.

I slid back to consciousness in a water bed which gurgled
rudely at the least movement. But that movement had to
come from other people, turning me occasionally like a spit
roast to ease the pain. It amused me, I remember, to discover that the only part of my body I could move at all was
the little finger of my right hand. I waggled it at Mother and
she waggled back. It seemed a childish performance but I
think it put guts into both of us.

There came the removal of my demi-carcase to Edinburgh's City Hospital from our house at 21 Pitt Street, and
for the first time in my life I was aware of being a public
spectacle. As I was stretchered down the steps, women with
mouths like empty shopping baskets lined the pavement
buying my discomfiture, using their round and shining eyes
as currency. I have seen such ladies since, clustered round
a street accident or a dying dog. I have seen their expression
mirrored by the inhabitants of the fishmonger's slab; but
the cod have at least the excuse of being dead. Some of us
spend our lives being odd, and heaven forbid we ever join
the gawking ranks of the even. Worse than pain, the blacksmith, is the agonizingly painless scrutiny of fish eyes.

In the City Hospital I was put on the danger list and given
an enema, a penny-whistle, a tray-cloth to embroider, and
a clarinet – all in that order. The least musical of these
instruments, as I remember, was the tray-cloth which was
given me to encourage the use of my nine futile fingers. The
enema – which Father insisted was in B flat – was for my

internal well-being. The other two pipes, applied at the other end, were provided to redevelop my breathing. Efforts to produce a tune restored my lung power in record time; but what effect this musical therapy had on other patients was carefully concealed from me.

Coaxed into the intricacies of button-hole, lazy daisy, moss and satin stitch, my fingers began to regain some dexterity. My speech which had also been paralysed recovered sufficiently for me to be able to ask what was wrong with me.

'Poliomyelitis,' my mother said lightly. 'It means that you won't be able to walk about for some time.'

'For how long?' I asked.

'Oh, a week or two, I would think,' she replied, but I knew from her expression that she was being evasive.

'We're sending you out to a hospital at Fairmilehead on the outskirts of Edinburgh.'

The Princess Margaret Rose Hospital had wards jutting from a main corridor like widely spaced teeth in a comb. Each ward had only three walls, and where the fourth might have been was open to the elements night and day. I found myself among some forty other boys, some suffering from TB, others from spina bifida, spastic paralysis and hip joint disease. Withered limbs, weighted with sandbags and iron, hung from Balkan beams, their tendons showing white through mottled skin. I do not know whether the name of the disease or the sight of some of the victims terrified me the more.

I was taken straight to the plaster room and swathed from head to toes in soggy, tepid bandages. The resultant hardened shell, placed on a bed across two orange boxes, became my home for the next three months. My arms were wired out straight on either side in what I can only describe as a Christlike attitude.

My ward-mates were mostly lads from poor homes, and when my mother arrived at visiting hour with a posy of flowers, their jeers and jibes had me blushing to the marrow of my bones. I tried desperately to pretend that, whoever she was, she didn't belong to me. But she kissed me on the forehead and I wished that I had the use of arms to pull the bedclothes over my head. Poor Mother could not understand: to be cosseted in that ward was to invite ridicule. In the interminable days that followed I dreaded the visits of my parents.

The posy of flowers brought by Mother, loathed though it was at the time, blossoms yet. It was given to her to bring to me by Hamish Paterson, an Edinburgh artist and friend of my father. The story of its gathering is a saga in itself.

Hamish had been in a pub when the news of my apparently imminent demise reached him: he had decided to drown his sadness and in mid-anaesthetic had remembered my love of colour and wild flowers. An exploding shell had blown off both his hands in the First World War but a field surgeon had somehow managed to stick them on again, more or less back to front. Despite this handicap he was an acredited master of his brushes.

And now he swallowed his last dram, borrowed a glass of water from the publican, and thus equipped set out on a taxi tour of the city. The floral composition he had in mind must range through all the colours of the spectrum. When he saw the shade of flower or weed he required, be it in a park, by the roadside or in somebody's garden, he would stop the taxi – and the driver obliged his every whim. Stuck for a few essential hues (it was late September) he rang an old woman's doorbell and asked if he might go through her darning basket. With his clumsy hands he fashioned wool into florettes for the centrepiece of his composition.

Hamish arrived at the hospital with his offering, but Authority disliked both his dishevelled appearance and Bacchic aroma, and forbade him access. And so he sought refuge with my mother. Would she kindly pay his taxi fare (£2 17s.) and had she anything in the house to eat, and if the police called would she assure them that he was relatively harmless? Never, surely, were flowers more dearly given.

No one, it seemed, knew much about polio in 1938 – at least not in Edinburgh. Warmth, movement and exercise constituted treatment in the US and Australia. But for me at least cold air and immobility were the orders of the day. My bed was wheeled into the open end of the ward, and as autumn turned to winter my misery increased. I remember one night of bitter cold when snow began to lie on my bed-mat and melt on my exposed arms. I begged to be moved to the heated end of the ward, but my pleas went unheeded. In the morning snow had drifted into the ward and sparrows and rooks were pecking crumbs in the shelter of the beds. Having feathers, I thought, had its advantages.

I could not feed myself, and even had I been able, I could not stomach the hospital diet. Stewed sausage and a sludge of cabbage in a cracked enamel dish were thrust at me by nurses who had little time to spare for fussy kids like me. My weight went down below five stone.

Mother kicked up hell with Mr Cochrane, the orthopaedic surgeon in charge. Why could I not have Bovril, Ovaltine and other nourishing beverages? His reply was that patent foods were a waste of time. The embers of life were burning pretty low, and I cared little whether I lived or died.

One of the doctors was a dark athletic man with a fearful speech impediment. He prefaced his remarks by making a noise rather like a sealion asking for fish. I asked him one evening when he thought I would be up and about again. His reply haunts me yet.

'Aah – aah – aah – aah – you will never walk again,' he said. At the time I was too stunned and too weak to feel much anger. But if I ever meet that man again, may there be friends beside me to restrain me from belting him one on his bedside manner.

If I were never to walk again, I argued to my parents, might I not be allowed to lie in the comfort of my own home? At least might I not spend Christmas there?

They put the question to Mr Cochrane. His reply was terse. 'If you take your son out of this hospital you may kill him.'

It is a tribute to their courage that they decided to take the gamble and bring me home for Christmas. Neither they nor I ever regretted it.

A blue budgerigar chuckled in a cage and three goldfish swam in their round glass world. My dog came to lick my hand and the touch of her long forgotten fur brought tears to my eyes. A fire burned in the grate and the smell of lentil broth crept upstairs from the kitchen and curled round my

70

heart. I ate my first full meal for three months and that night I slept in a warm bed. But the damage had already been done. Cold, immobility and undernourishment had taken their toll, and a year and four months were to pass before I began learning to walk all over again. Had home treatment begun sooner I am certain my recovery would have been fuller and more rapid.

At the beginning of the following summer Father rented a house with a garden at Roslin, on the outskirts of Edinburgh, and on fine days I was allowed to lie outside on a camp bed. My most prized possession was a telescope, powerful enough to bring wild birds, far hills and even the early moon into sharp focus. My small and restricted world expanded greatly.

From town one day my father brought a red kite with 1500 feet of string. I think he derived even more pleasure from it than did I; and so successful was its maiden flight that windy August that he bought a further 1500 feet of string. Getting the kite airborne above the trees, he allowed me to pay out most of the 3000 feet. The pull on my arms seemed enormous but such exercise was theraputic. The kite soared, a red blob in a starling's egg sky, flying perhaps at a height of 500 feet. Out of the thin blue a biplane droned, heading straight for our toy.

We watched spellbound as the pilot banked and circled, inspecting it carefully. He then flattened out and, apparently following the white string, zoomed in low over our garden. We waved to him but he did not wave back. Within half an hour a police car was at our door.

What, an officer demanded, did Father think he was doing? Father in turn inquired if there were a law against flying a kite – and couldn't the police go and fly their own?

They were not pleased. Rumours of impending war were rife. Our kite had been reported flying close to a munitions factory. The RAF had been alerted and, in turn, the police. And now they wanted to know Father's name, nationality, occupation, political affiliations, blood group and size in socks. Fortunately his status with the BBC stood him in good stead, and the police were quickly able to check that he was not an enemy agent but a mere mad musician.

The declaration of war and the proximity of the munitions factory prompted Father to evacuate Mother and myself to my aunt's house in the quiet Perthshire village of Muthill, and thence to another rented house in the township of Crieff. Once more I was in sight of mountains.

The view from our front windows in Carrington Terrace commanded upper Strathearn, burning then with the cold fires of autumn. Flames of copper, cramesy and lemon licked along the valley, and white with early snow against a darker sky stood the peaks of Glen Artney. Skimming down the strath one vivid day came an arrowhead of Spitfires, tight as the ace of spades. Their grace and swallow swiftness made me long to be flying with them, free from the chafing constriction of a plaster shell. That longing became an actual ache and to ease the ache I knew I had to put that glimpse of power and freedom into words. I began to write:

> *Spitfire, sloping to the pinpoint of infinity,*
> *Bird shadow leaping the brazen crags*
> *Where only the wind sings,*
> *No birdsong, breaking from the woods of dawn,*
> *Could fill me full of such celestial joy.*

What a sickening lump of sugar that seems now! It tried to borrow something, I think, from Stephen Spender's *Express* (then the greatest poem ever penned). There was a second stanza to this effusion too, but mercifully for all concerned I have forgotten how it ran.

But that glutinous poem convinced me of one thing: if it happened that I would never walk hill or moorland again, at least I might be able to fly (Douglas Bader's example was to reinforce that notion) and if flying failed I would still be able to write. I found the thought comforting. As it transpired, I was writing long before I first tried to fly, and the latter experience I found rather unnerving.

Towards the end of 1939 the BBC Scottish Orchestra and my father were transferred from Edinburgh to the studios at Queen Margaret Drive, Glasgow. The move put them some forty miles further from Germany but, as it happened, into one of the Luftwaffe's target areas. There was solace, however, in the thought that their new headquarters was reasonably bomb-proof. Mother and I came to Glasgow at Christmas and a new orthopaedic specialist came into my life.

Sandy Miller was a rugged man, topping six feet in height. Black eyebrows met across the bridge of his nose in happy companionship. His eyes were a piercing blue and a stubborn jut of chin kept levering his mouth into a boyish grin. He thought he could put me back on my feet.

I was installed in an annexe of the Victoria Infirmary at Langside, one of a ward of four. Balkan beams were hoisted around my bed and an intensive course of exercises began, my withered limbs supported by slings. Mr Miller watched my progress with grinning satisfaction, but he was among the first to admit that a rebellious fellow patient contributed as much as anyone to my rehabilitation.

Into our ward one night there walked a young man suffering from an excruciating headache. Despite the pain, he sat up in bed, lit a forbidden cigarette and told us an extraordinary story.

'Chuck' Pinkerton owned rhubarb fields at Millerston to the north-east of Glasgow. In addition to this peaceful profession he was a speedway rider, part-time diver for the Royal Navy and a titled boxer. He had been riding his motor cycle one Sunday on his way to a diving job when he stopped to allow churchgoers to cross the street.

'A car following me crashed right into my back,' he said. 'The impact knocked me straight into the air. I remember just missing the overhead tram cables before landing on the street in a sitting position. Fortunately I was wearing a thick diving suit at the time.'

Even so, a man of lesser fitness and physique might have been fatally injured. He counted himself lucky to have escaped with a sore head. Headache or not, he found lying in bed a complete bore. All attempts to keep him between the sheets were doomed to failure. A scolding from one of our prettier nurses – a lass from Lithuania – demanded prompt revenge.

Leaping from bed, Chuck armed himself with a soda water syphon and waited for Nurse Valita's re-entry to our ward. Foster-mothering was not one of her duties, but never have I seen such a wet nurse! Excited by the general hilarity, I joined battle by hurling some over-ripe plums at her assailant. His reaction was instantaneous. Scraping the fruit from his person, he snatched back my bedclothes and rammed the pulpy mass down the hole in my plaster shell which allowed my stomach to expand after mealtimes.

The second battle of Langside was ended by the dramatic entrance of Sister herself. Mr Pinkerton was threatened with expulsion, but it in no way quelled his zest for physical activity.

Slipping from bed one night, he stole from the ward, found his clothes in the locker room, dressed and went out. His absence was not noticed and he managed to return undetected and bearing gifts. He had bought chocolates, cigarettes for himself; two soft rubber golf balls for me, some cord and some string.

'We'll get to work with those in the morning,' he said enigmatically. When morning arrived he stripped to his pyjama bottoms and advanced upon me flexing magnificent muscles. He found a length of blind cord, exhaled and tied it round his chest. With tremendous panache he breathed in – and the tough cord burst asunder. Knotting the remainder round his upper arm, he performed a similar feat with his biceps.

'That shows you the capabilities of the human body,' he announced. 'I will now tie some string around your biceps and you will try to break it.'

The thin string cut into my arm and did not burst, so now I had to squeeze the rubber golf balls in my hands, and between my biceps and forearms. This, he explained, was how to build mighty muscles – a far better developer than any doctor's namby-pamby exercise. We were too engrossed to notice that two people were watching and listening interestedly – Mr Miller and Matron no less.

'I think, Mr Pinkerton, that you had better return to bed,' said Matron acidly. But for once Mr Pinkerton had a champion.

'Just a minute,' said Sandy Miller. 'These golf balls might not be a bad idea.' He felt Chuck's massive arm appreciatively. 'Yes,' he said, 'Don could certainly do with some of that. See to it, though, that he doesn't overdo it.'

So peace returned to the ward. And in the days to follow

I practised squeezing golf balls and bursting string like mad: the development of my chest and arms seemed almost miraculous. At the end of three months I was being levered out of bed, a caliper on each leg and a spinal jacket to support my back.

My first tentative steps were agonizing. Polio had contorted my toes. The unaccustomed rush of blood to my feet caused my legs to swell like sausages. Worst of all, I had been 4 feet 10 inches in 1938, and now in April 1940, I surveyed a slippery polished floor from the giddy height of 5 feet 8 inches. Vertigo spun me like a top – and has been my enemy ever since, ready to sneak up on me when least expected.

With a nurse tucked under each armpit I made my tottering way into the corridor, and the sight which met my eyes I will never forget. An elderly man in a dressing gown was passing, his leg swathed in bandages, in line astern behind him there came a procession of hospital cats. Apparently the dressing on his affliction smelled of fish. Every so often he would turn round and say, 'Fissssst' very loudly; but the ratcatchers of the Victorian Order followed him with tails at the salute.

Despite my own problems I was nearly helpless with laughter. I was giggling still when I hirpled into a women's ward. Some of the ladies were kind enough to applaud my entry, and the welcome must have gone to my head. Crossing my left leg over my right, I relinquished my nurses and smashed to the floor. The impact was as nothing compared to the shrieking agony in my groins. The ring tops of my calipers had crossed with the savagery of nutcrackers and my soprano screech might well have become a permanent vocal characteristic. Why this first accident had to happen in a women's ward is a subject I have often pondered. Suffice to say that my torture evoked a sympathetic sigh from the ladies present.

I found myself in sympathy with the Aberdeenshire farmer who, pub conversation claims, was unlucky enough to be travelling in a train compartment behind three women bent on discussing the most painful moments of their married lives. Difficult labour, the birth of twins and prolapses of the womb were discussed in awful detail while the farmer cringed behind his newspaper.

Feeling eventually that he should perhaps contribute to – and even end – the discussion, he said: 'Excuse me, ladies, but have ony o' ye ever been kickit in the ba's by a stallion?'

This story belongs to the rich earth of my native county. Vulgar it may be in a modern age which has discovered the horrors of sex and the bathos of women's liberation, but so far as I am concerned it puts the differences between man and woman in decent perspective. The dung midden is never to be despised when it grows healthy crops.

Vulgarity and pornography for their own sake are, I think, as unpleasant, unethical and unpractical as sharn on a carpet. Any good man of the soil will tell you that the drawing room is no place for growing crops – any more than the fertile field is the proper place for industrial waste or pop festivals. Emancipators may scream for freedom of expression, the liberation of this or that. A Buchan ploughman could lose them in vocabulary – and yet blush at using four-letter words in public. There is a time, a place and a use for everything.

Leonardo's Leda and the Swan is not pornographic: it is exonerated by its superb and sympathetic drawing. It is the drawing and not the subject which matters. What the butler saw is liable to be pure porn. He shouldn't have been looking anyway and the subject is not to inspire, but to arouse baser instincts. Blatant crudity on stage or on TV creates a furore because the audience is heterogeneous, and to insist sex on such an audience is a mild form of rape. When good sense, humour and taste prevail, censorship should not be necessary.

The business of learning to balance and keep upright made me realize quickly that it was first of all imperative to learn how to fall without hurting myself. I practised by allowing myself to topple forwards first of all against a bed, and then a cushion on the floor, and finally the floor itself. This exercise is not to be recommended for the faint of heart, but it is certainly a safeguard against broken limbs. And having once learned to topple to the ground like a falling tree, I had to learn how to get back up again.

This, I discovered, was impossible from a level surface. Like the long-winged swift I was pretty helpless on the ground. Some prop such as a chair or table leg was needed with which to hoist myself up. For long enough I had nightmares about falling on flat desert ground without a point of leverage for miles around.

Finally I learned to walk supporting myself on two sticks, remembering that if any crossing were to be done it should be with fingers and not legs. Mr Cochrane was invited from Edinburgh for my first solo performance. He seemed astounded, and even complimented my mother on the fine job she had made of me. But how I wished that his stammering henchmen had been there: I would have relinquished both sticks to be able to thumb my nose at him.

I was given a final muscle count – left leg 30 per cent of normal, right leg 10 per cent. Thanks to my friend Chuck, his string and golf balls, I had, apart from a few missing muscles, arms of a strength above average. Thus equipped for adventurous living, I was sent home to our new abode in the west end of Glasgow.

Life became one long holiday. Clouston Street in the early forties was merry with children of my own age, and I had a lot of fun to catch up on. Hide and seek, cops and robbers and cowboys and Indians were favourite games; not the least reason being that they afforded one the opportunity to linger for a few moments in a quiet corner with the girl of one's transient fancy.

Becoming mobile was of paramount importance and towards that end I constructed a vehicle called bogie, hurlie, cartie or coaster, depending on where you were brought up. My pals towed me along to the nearest steep hill, gave me a shove, and all those wasted weeks and months flashed into insignificance as gravity took hold of my wheels. I was in command of the hurtling road to glory, wind on my cheek and imagined Messerschmitts in my sights. I was a hell-bent Spitfire, a howling Hurricane – but the immediate and unintentional target was an elderly person in an elderly Ford, turning the corner at the bottom.

I swerved and the tyres of my bogie's pram wheels sundered. I must have been doing 40 m.p.h. when I hit a lamp-post dislocating my left elbow.

The pain was much less than I deserved, and helping hands wrenching me to my feet, managed to locate what had been dislodged and rehouse it, smarting, in the joint it was used to occupying. My furtive flight towed their squadron leader home on wobbling wheels.

Mother was sweet about the whole thing. If that was the way I chose to kill myself, well – carry on. My friends were not at all to blame, and she thanked them for bringing me home. Greatly relieved, they scampered off to recount their adventure and were astounded to get the telling-off of their lives. Aiding and abetting in the further crippling of cripples is frowned on by society.

Ridding myself of surgical appliances now occupied my attention. Clanking around with nearly a stone of ironmongery and leatherwork was hot and uncomfortable work in summer. By bandaging my left knee I managed to walk without a caliper, and in a mood of reckless abandon, left off my spinal jacket. Like an idiot I took my new-found freedom for a walk and only just managed to limp home. I was warned that going about without a spinal brace would result in the serious curvature of my backbone – and so it did. But it was better than being encased like a mummy.

As my activeness increased, I gained notoriety at the infirmary workshop as a smasher of calipers. 'They are not designed for climbing trees or hopping over walls,' I was told. My reply to that, which I was not brave enough to mutter aloud, was, 'Well, they bloody well should be!' With armaments devouring all metal available, I suppose I was fortunate to have a caliper at all, but the cast iron used was real rubbish. I got fed up having to be spot-welded.

On a fishing trip with Father at Donside, Aberdeenshire, I broke my caliper crossing a ditch, and where in the wilderness could a repair be affected? Father fortunately remembered that the hamlet of Bellabeg boasted a smiddy and took me there. A huge Clydesdale filled the doorway, patiently awaiting pedicure. The smith did not bat an eyelid on being asked to mend my broken support.

'Ye'll just ha'e tae wait while the cuddy gets his shoes,' he said.

What a blessed sense of priorities that man had! We watched in fascination as bellows roused his forge to a roaring red, as sparks glanced between hammer head and shoe. The smith's art is a symphony for the five senses. The eye drinks in the elemental fantasy of fire. The ear rejoices with the anvil. Skin glows in the warmth of the forge. The smell of old leather, horse and singeing hoof sings in the nostrils and tingles, I swear, on the taste buds. My father, remembering his ancestry, was thrilled.

When the horse was comfortable in his new hot shoes, it came my turn. With something approaching awe I saw my caliper thrust into the heart of the forge. Somehow its leather did not even singe. A few hammer blows and the job was done.

'Ca' that half-a-croon,' said the smith; but my father gave him ten shillings to cover the cost of our entertainment. That caliper in its lifetime never broke again.

Even when a new support was prescribed I felt reluctant to throw old faithful away; it had too much magic forged into its ugly form.

7

If You Can't Join Them

The sudden sound of the chord of B minor was enough to make my father jump like a stag – a reflex occasioned by the fact that the notes of the air raid siren were B and D. This mournful minor third affected him even long after the Second World War was over. Perfect pitch was sometimes an absolute menace. Again, when the drone of an aircraft filled the night sky, his critical ear enabled him to distinguish 'one of theirs' from 'one of ours'. War was inescapable.

During one raid on Clydeside in 1941 he donned his Home Guard's tin hat and went to conduct the war from our front doorstep. For his pains he was struck on the lid by a piece of falling shrapnel which ricocheted and hit a half-grown kitten which happened to be passing our gate. Poor puss was carried in with a large lump swelling up on his back, and nursing him took Father's mind off hostilities other than the collision of consecutive fifths.

An extraordinary *rapport* developed between man and cat. The animal treated Mother with disdain – probably because she insisted on christening him Chloe – but it adored its rescuer. One day it followed him to the BBC. In No. 1 Studio he was about to raise his baton to start rehearsal when sixty players began giggling behind their stands.

Tartly, Father inquired if he might be allowed in on the joke. 'The joke,' said Jack Begbie, leader of the orchestra, 'is sitting right behind you.'

Shortly afterwards a neighbour of ours was surprised to find herself accosted on Queen Margaret Bridge by a distraught conductor bearing a handful of black and white kitten.

'Kindly put this in your shopping basket and deliver it to my wife,' he ordered, and the lady was too astonished to refuse. It was not very long until puss was back again at the BBC, a refugee of the Clydebank blitz.

We were sheltering in our hall, Mother, Father, cat and dog, when the raid began. Sometime around midnight the loudest explosion imaginable blasted in all our windows.

Minutes later there was another heavy thud and a voice in the street crying, 'Landmine! – evacuate your houses – evacuate!' Terror almost induced us to obey in another sense of the word. The scene which met us at the front door was frightful. Clouston Street was ankle deep in broken glass and rubble. A lurid fire blazed at the far end of the street. My father decided to make for the relatively bomb-proof safety of the BBC, some quarter-of-a-mile away. Mother made the journey in dressing gown and slippers carrying Sheila, our Cairn terrier. I travelled on Father's back, somehow clutching our petrified cat. We made a strange procession.

The sight which seared my eyes remains vivid after thirty years. A corner house was blazing strenuously, lighting up the scene. A Rolls-Royce, almost two-dimensional, was plastered against a tenement wall like some macabre poster. My father stumbled and slithered over what had once been a living person. High in a tree beside the BBC a little dog hung suspended by its lead, walks over. An armchair and a sewing machine teetered on the parapet of the bridge spanning the Kelvin. As we passed the blazing house its roof collapsed with a crackling roar, drowning every sound except the screaming of those inside. Until that moment the war had seemed a kind of rough, impersonal game played by distant combatants. We were thankful to reach the sanctuary of the BBC's solid basement.

It was two days before we were allowed home. Lying on an army lorry outside our house was the unexploded land-mine which had necessitated our departure. It was over eleven feet long and weighed more than a ton and a half. Our informant was a red-haired Army bomb disposal expert who, I remember was happily, and I think necessarily, under the influence of drink.

'Look at the beauty,' he grinned. 'Good job for us she's

a dud. Made in Czechoslovakia,' he added significantly.

The mine, apparently aimed at Kirklee Bridge, some fifty yards distant had crashed through the roof of a boarding house nearly opposite our home. A dear old soul was surprised when it smashed through the ceiling of her top floor bedroom. Clambering over it, she had trotted downstairs and announced to her landlady, 'Do you know, dear, something terrible has happened? One of the chimneys has fallen into my room.'

In such ways does heaven protect the innocent from knowing too much of what is going on.

The Clydebank blitz was directly responsible for my being packed off to Coldingham in Berwickshire where my Aunt Eliza now owned a small hotel. My joy knew no bounds at being with my cousin George again, and being introduced to his pet owl, Jacob II. Feeding him in wartime proved difficult. Mice and rats were not rationed and required no coupons, but George no longer had a retrieving cat. Traps and human strategy had to be employed, and in Jacob's latter years I remember Old Bella, the daily help and treasure, arriving at the hotel at 7 a.m. with a carrier bag labelled Younger's Ale.

'My, Bella,' I said, 'you're early on the road with your carry-out.'

'It's no my cairry-oot,' she protested indignantly. 'It's a poke of mice I catchit for the burrrd.'

George's uncle John Quarry was staying at the hotel with his black Labrador. Despite his fierce moustache and chancy temper the retired policeman and I became firm friends, and Drake was the most sagacious dog this side of Ancient Greece.

'Bring my bunnet and boots and we'll go for a stroll,' Uncle John would say: the dog would mouth his cap from its peg, place it on his master's head and go for the boots.

'That's the left boot – I want the right one,' Uncle John would say in mock exasperation, and the beast would rectify the error. My first walk with them was an eye-opener in owner-dog relationship.

Half a mile away from home old John said, 'Dammit, Drake, I've left my pipe and baccy on the kitchen table' –

and in a flash the great black animal was racing down the road.

'Watch this,' John said when Drake was out of sight, and he threw a box of matches into the ditch. We walked on in silence. Presently the pounding of feet announced the dog's arrival, pipe and tobacco pouched in his soft jaws.

John patted first the dog and then his pockets. 'Strange,' quoth he, 'I seem to have dropped my matches somewhere.'

I stood spellbound as Drake zig-zagged away, back-tracking John's scent, finally plunging into the ditch and emerging triumphantly with the matches. Such intelligence required more than Drake's exquisite sense of smell.

The only trouble dog ever gave master happened on the day a telegram came telling John that his son Joe had been severely wounded in the Middle East.

'Alice, my housekeeper, was standing beside me when I read out the message,' Uncle John told me. 'She fainted at the news. The dog thought I had struck her, and came straight for my throat.

'I had just time to dodge and give him the most almighty thud on the lug. "Learn to read, you bugger," I told him, and he was sick for days at the thought of what he'd nearly done.'

George kept dogs of his own and one of them, a fox and Border terrier crossed puppy, had the misfortune to break his foreleg. The nearest vet was miles away and no transport was available. I had to treat him myself. The fracture, hospital experience told me, was greenstick, and I thought a splint would suffice – but what to use? My eyes fell on a length of garden hose, roughly the thickness of the puppy's paw. I cut off about three inches and slit it down one side. Giving the pup a bowl of warm milk laced with brandy as anaesthetic, I applied the rubber splint and bound it tight. To my delight, this expedient worked. Despite the momentary pain I had occasioned him, he became my faithful follower, never allowing me out of sniffing distance. At Coldingham the war seemed far away, but the pup and I were due to come under fire.

On a headland above the village one day in early summer I heard the sound of an aircraft flying low. I looked up nonchalantly – and was startled out of my skin to see a Junkers 88 flying seawards, crosses and swastikas clearly visible overhead. A machine gun began to chatter, but I was already in a hedge-bottom with the pup in my arms. As the noise of the plane receded, the sound of a second engine grew in volume, that of a Hurricane, hot in pursuit. Out in a grey shroud of North Sea haar a short burst of gunfire sounded, nails in a coffin, holes drilled perhaps in a road which needed a lot of mending.

I was on my feet, bleeding, when the Hurricane returned performing victory rolls above a limping, yelling boy and a limping, barking pup. It was something of an anti-climax to discover that the blood on my hands and face had not been honourably won. A wild rose had sheltered me, and her thorns had been fierce in protection.

St Abbs fishermen brought in the German dead some days later to their land rest. Those same men, or their sons, or kindred fishers, buried my cousin George thirty years later in the same red Berwickshire earth. And the gulls wailed as much for the one as for the others, and the seasons did not fail to roll round, and the minister was drowned out by the lark.

For almost two years now I had had little in the way of schooling other than the occasional visits of a kindly tutor whose pet subject was English. A few brief weeks at Glasgow High School, a labrinth of awkward stairways, proved too much for me physically. Father determined to pack me off to Dollar Academy in the quiet countryside of Clackmannanshire. I was dumped into the second year at the age of sixteen, an ignominy which I felt keenly at the time. Even now I have a recurring dream in which I am sent to school again to repeat the same performance.

At Dollar I was put in the care of a stout, matriarchal landlady with a heart of honey. Mrs Mac (the 'tavish' ending was never used) was a strong woman, adored by her friends and dreaded by her few enemies. She had spent most of her married life in Argentina where Jock, her husband, was in charge of railway development. For the sake of their sons' education they had retired to Dollar.

Their two younger sons were wild to say the least. The

sibilant swish of the tawse pursued their erratic passage through school, but to everyone's amazement they made good in the Mercantile Service.

Rationing was iron hard in Dollar, but Mrs Mac had a magical way of keeping the larder stocked. Almost every day of the week she performed a kind of loaves and fishes miracle, and lads from neighbouring boarding houses were never denied a bite to eat. Smoking was forbidden by the school rules, but not by Mrs Mac. Her house, as a result was scarcely ever empty.

My room-mate was a lad from Kinross, Jack Wood, about 5 feet 4 inches in height and scarcely less, it seemed, across the shoulders. Stripping off for bed at night, he would flex his muscles and perform such feats as lifting his iron bedstead between his teeth. Boxing was his great delight and he kept trying to get me to spar with him. I managed to fob him off until one night he pinned me in a corner and demanded that I defend myself. Several times he cuffed me about the ears and my normally placid nature came to the boil. I waited, ready for his next lunge, and, as he came forward, hit him with all my power flush on the chin. He crumpled to the floor, blood trickling from his mouth.

'Mrs Mac,' I yelled in a kind of sobbing unbelief, 'I think I've killed Jack.'

She inspected his sleeping form and sponged his face, but it was fully five minutes before he came round. He did not offer to spar with me again.

Like Glasgow High School, Dollar Academy was fraught with stairways. Unlike some sophisticated institutes, we did not sit on our bottoms awaiting a succession of teachers: the teachers stayed put, and we, as I think was right, had to do the scuttling around.

The route from 'Peerie' Walton's English classroom to 'Willie B' Sproat's history class lay right round the main school building and up a flight of stairs. Mr Sproat did not like latecomers and Mr Walton would not countenance early leavers. Asking a pal to carry my books, I would attempt a kind of lurching sprint from class to class to be in time, but I was always late for history.

As I panted into the room Mr Sproat would look at his

watch and say ,'Congratulations – you've knocked ten seconds off your record.' Such gentle sarcasm made me resolve to beat the clock. I never did – but the therapy was excellent.

Dollar was good for me. We were expected to wear open-necked shirts in winter as in summer. Ties were reserved for Sundays and pullovers for the thin of skin. Under the green-grey Ochil Hills I felt my lungs expanding and my mental powers, numbed and neglected for four years, beginning to revive.

The minister at St Columba's Church was the Rev. Thomas Stobo Glen, an extraordinary man with the most extraordinary tales to tell. His parrot's beak curved down below a balding crown, and the ends of his long white hair were stained, I think, with nicotine. He had the habit of arriving punctually at tea time, and one cup was enough to inspire his reminiscences.

I vividly remember his tale of tonsillectomy. He had had a sore throat, he told us, and diagnosing the trouble correctly, had decided to be his own surgeon. Standing before a mirror, he had propped his mouth open with matchsticks and performed the operation with a razor blade. No flicker of an eyelid, I swear, betrayed that he was telling us anything but the gospel truth. But his tonsils took a bit of swallowing.

At a sheep sale in Perth, he averred, he had once been silly enough to raise his hat to a lady he recognized. The auctioneer, mistaking the gesture, had knocked down to him forty-two black-faced lambs.

Accepting his lot graciously, he had paid up and arranged for the animals to be put in his glebe. On visits to neighbouring farms he had asked for sustenance for his flock. The turnips given him had fattened his lambs, and at season's end he had sold them at a profit.

Listening to Mr Stobo Glen's tales, told with such candour and conviction, gave strange credence to Bible stories of greater antiquity. He was after all, a man of God; and God, we knew, moved in mysterious ways. . . .

Fishing, more than anything else, helped to restore my sense of balance and improve my physique. Mrs Mac's sister Sheena and her mother lived at the schoolhouse in Glendevon, less than ten miles from Dollar, and the brown, murmuring river ran at their back door. Old Mrs Blair was the kindest and most gentle of Highlandwomen. Never once did I hear voice raised in rebuke or anger: she loved the world and the world loved her in return.

Griddle scones thick with butter and golden syrup awaited my arrival off the Crieff bus. Like a good working cat I was never allowed to go hunting on an empty stomach.

In the rippling river, small trout, dappled black and gold, quivered in their runs and eddies. Stone flies hatched under boulders. Olives lived out their brief, mouthless life cycles where beech fronds nodded above the stream. Breathless with eagerness, I stumbled through thickets and over boulders to reach that enchanted waterside. Obstacles became as nothing where there were rising fish in sight. I learned to cast a dry fly just upstream of every questing nose and flickering tail. Willow wrens wheepled in bush and briar and cock chaffinches chuckled 'Very, very, very, very pleased to meetcha.' Fishing I may have been, but my mind was busy trying to pour back something of the pleasure cup I was so greedily drinking.

Writing poetry, I was beginning to find, was a necessary ingredient of life. It was as if, having been mated with the world around, one had to gestate and labour and finally give birth to a child in the image of its sire. Usually, as far as I was concerned, the offspring was a pretty poor reflection of its parent, and I lived in envy of the masters of their trade. I fed myself on Shakespeare, Milton, Wordsworth and Tennyson, hoping to extract the magic elixir which made them worthy of memory, but is was like watching bees at work, seeing tongues and wings and hairy knees employed – and yet learning little or nothing about honey-making.

Fishing, I discovered, had less to do with the catching of fish than with the joy of water glitter, the turning of a leaf, the glistering path of snails or the clattering of a beetle's wing. But to return from the river bank, clean of fish, was to invite the ridicule of every man without music in his soul. Women were even worse critics, and I am certain their attitude is a legacy from cave dwelling days when the hunter, returning empty handed, was an object of derision.

The men who really knew how to wile trout from the

Devon hailed from places like Sauchie and Tullibody. Characters like Auld Andra and the Piper would leave their homes on a Friday night and trudge five miles into the Ochils to reach the source of the river. Auld Andra was known to wrap himself up in his threadbare coat and huddle on the hillside waiting for the morning rise. He was over eighty at the time.

Those dedicated souls would fish downstream to Frandy reservoir and thence down Glen Devon to the Tormaukin Inn in time for a pint before the last bus home on a Saturday evening. I have seen that bus so crowded with fishers that once one of them had to make the journey sitting on the front wing hanging on to a headlamp.

On that occasion the Piper (not even he knew how the nickname derived) was visibly under the influence. A lurch of the bus caused him to stagger and a cascade of wet trout slithered from his basket on to a woman's lap. Her shrieks of anguish and the Piper's tipsy apologies made comedy of the highest rustic order.

The Piper it was who taught me the art of the dry fly. I almost fell over him one day when he was lurking behind a bush by the river.

'Hae ye mony troots the day?' he squeaked at me.

'None, I'm afraid,' I said sadly.

He removed his bonnet, extracted a handful of feathers, and bound one round a tiny hook.

'Pit that on your cast,' he ordered, 'and flick it oot ahint yon stane.'

I did as I was bidden and from the thinnest water imaginable a fat half-pounder leaped, was played and landed. The Piper's weird fly accounted for another five fish that joyous morning.

The summer white of the rowans ripened into rich red. The first frosts gripped the earth with iron fists. Autumn yielded to winter and one day after a heavy snowfall, the mercury had hardly the strength to rise. The temperature lay at two degrees Fahrenheit and the snow became like white and shining rock. At night a full moon, rising on this whiteness, seemed to turn darkness into day. My friends resolved to go sledging. I longed to accompany them, but walking uphill on ice and frozen snow was impossible for me. And then one lad came up with a brilliant idea. If I were to sit on one sledge and tow the others behind me, the rest of the boys would form a team and haul me up the hill.

I donned two pairs of trousers, several sweaters and a Balaclava helmet, and our procession of twenty set out, breaths smoking in the aching, arid air. Our route lay up the Burnside through Dollar's old town where the winding road had a gradient of one in eight. Beyond the last houses my panting team trudged on sliding, rasping boots. We filed through a gateway into a sloping field and turned to survey the world around and below us.

Under that rolling moon and a vast parabola of stars it was possible to see out of our county into the neighbouring shires of Perth and Fife. And there in this high field we faced a downhill run of well over a mile. The thought of the steep icy bends through the old town made me shiver, but now was no time for panic. Two of my mates set off before me to act as a sort of reception committee at journey's end. And now I lay prone above keen steel runners, wished myself luck and plunged downhill.

The first half-mile was uneventful and gave me time to practise steering and braking with the toes of either shoe. And then the steepness of the old town sucked me down like a matchstick in a whirlpool. I must have been doing well over 40 m.p.h., my face skimming a blur of singing ice. I tried to steer but could not. I ricocheted from a wall in a shower of sparks, whether from runners or caliper I neither knew nor cared.

As I hurtled headlong down the steepest part, an old man hove into view dragging a sledge on which reposed a sack of potatoes. He was dead in my path and I yelled like a dervish. He stared for a second then leaped for his life. My front runners sliced into his sack and I overturned in a welter of sledges and King Edwards. Fortunately he was disposed to regard youth as a necessary evil, and we helped him to gather up the remains of his scattered tatties.

We repeated our nerve tingling descent several times. Its dangers could not have been much less than those of the Cresta Run, and how none of us was injured or even killed

I will never know. For our finale we came down in crocodile formation, each lad holding fast to the sledge in front. It was decreed that, for reasons of safety, I would be tail-end Charlie. But no one told me that the effect of such a formation is to increase speed and also produce a vicious pendulum swing to the crocodile's tail. Half-way down I lost my sledge and finished the journey on my stomach. It was not until reaching home base that the dishevelment of my person became apparent. I had no buttons left on my jacket and few on the fly of my outer trousers. Worse still, the toe caps were worn completely out of my shoes.

Mrs Mac was pretty furious, but I think that even she derived secret pleasure from seeing my honourable scars. Not one of us had escaped bruising and Jack Wood resembled a walking icicle, having crashed his sledge through the frozen Dollar Burn.

That night's adventure, more, I think, than any other, served to put me on almost equal terms with my schoolmates. Gone for once was the incessant, nagging feeling of being odd man out. Lack of mobility is the obvious curse of having polio, but far worse is lack of participation. Dollar helped to build up every muscle left available to me and my mind sharpened commensurately. In the four years I spent there I managed to catch up on more than three wasted years away from school. It shamed me a bit to realize that I was over twenty when I gained my Higher Leaving Certificate. But at least schooldays were now behind me and I could look forward to whatever a wider world had to offer.

I had as yet no clear idea of what I wanted to do. I had long since had to abandon any idea of making a living from the land, although my passion for the Scottish countryside remained as strong as ever. On some days I was obsessed with the desire to write music, desperately trying to hear chords and counterpoints in my head without recourse to the piano, and wishing that I had inherited my father's talent. On other days painting landscapes and wildlife filled my hours; and on others still the need to write filled my mind with a consuming fire. The three arts, jockeying for position, kept cannoning into each other to their detriment. My particular dilemma had a tricorn head.

Mother was adamant that I should go to university. She argued that this would give me time to make up my mind about a career. I could not very well dispute her good sense, but somehow I felt that I was heading for a cul-de-sac in which teaching was the only possible profession, and the idea did not appeal.

On the other hand, the arts seemed to offer only a precarious livelihood and I was utterly determined to become self-supporting. While I pondered the possibilities my schooldays ended – but not without a frightening confrontation with authority.

An Army jeep was parked outside Mrs Mac's house as I lumbered home from school that last summer. Two unsmiling redcaps stopped me as I turned in at the gate and asked me if, by chance, my name happened to be Whyte.

One of the policemen began to reel off a list of charges. I had failed to report under such-and-such Conscription Act at Stirling Castle. I was accordingly in desertion, caught Absent without Leave, *in flagrante delicto*, in breach of this and in defiance of that. I was now, therefore, to be placed under close arrest and marched off to jankers.

Only then I remembered having received a yellow official form some weeks before, giving me the option of going down the mines or joining the Argylls. So amused was I to think that a crock like myself could be called up that I had burned it.

'At least let me tell my landlady that I'm under arrest,' I pleaded. Grudgingly they agreed, frog-marched me to the house and stood guard at the door. I blurted out my plight to Mrs Mac who swelled her outraged bosom like a brigadier and strode to my defence.

'If the Army thinks it has nothing better to do than call up cripples it wants its head examined,' she announced. Her house was her castle and she was darned if she was going to be assailed by troops, and they could go and raffle themselves.

She won the battle and the day. But it took teachers' and doctors' certificates and angry exchanges between Dollar and Stirling Castle before I got off the hook.

Revenge, however, is as sweet as saccharine. One of our last school ploys was to creep into an Army encampment in a nearby field and cut down the guy ropes at dead of night. I was proud to act as watch to my fellows, and satisfied to hear the startled yells of the victims.

Some of them were Poles, immaculately uniformed and mannered gentlemen who were not above paying court to our Dollar girls. One handsome officer aboard the bus to Tillicoultry gave up his seat to a comely lass and made a magnificent flourish. Priding himself on his grasp of English, he said, for all the bus to hear, 'Madame – kindly park your arse.'

But my belligerent attitude to Our Glorious Victors stemmed, if truth be told, from sheer jealously. There is nothing I would have enjoyed better than the right to wear a uniform sporting the wings of the RAF.

My former schoolmate Tom Hetherington flew over in his Barracuda dive-bomber one summer day when we were having tea in the garden. He came peeling out of the sky, screaming about the life which is death, and pulling away again just above our heads. And the starlings in the apple tree above us dropped into our laps and perched on teacups for an instant of bewildered time. I sat in an agony of envy and stared at the empty sky, painfully aware of my leaden legs, listening to the departing roar of power and freedom. And I think it was then that a new philosophy became quite clear in my mind; if you can't join them – beat them.

8

In Search of Independence

In the March of 1947 my father was invited to Norway to conduct the radio orchestra of that country, based in Oslo. As my university course did not start until the following autumn, I was allowed to accompany my parents.

Sailing from Newcastle, we arrived in Bergen and prepared to make the rail journey 250 miles through the mountains to our destination. Norway at the time was still bravely recovering from the effects of German occupation: the strain of these years of privation showed on more than a few faces.

The northland was still in the grip of winter and the railway carriage we boarded, commandeered from German stock, was heated like an oven. Figures huddled in furs sat in stifling compartments and no attempt on our part would induce them to shut off steam. In Norway 'ventilation' and 'draught' were synonymous and, surprisingly for a healthy race, people seemed to live between the two extremes of excessive natural cold outside and excessive artificial heat inside. Not long after the train had started we decided to go in search of cooler climes. But one of the hazards of this journey was the business of crossing from one coach to the next. In Britain I was used to passing through a kind of shoogly concertina with handrails. But on this infernal train we had to cross a sort of wobbling drawbridge with nothing in particular to hang on to.

Father walked the plank first and I brought up the rear. Having to watch my feet, I could not help but look down abysses hundreds of feet deep where rivers roared through caverns of rock and ice. I tried looking skywards, but the upper horizon was wild with mountains whose jagged peaks seemed to be toppling down on us. Vertigo, that terrier, shook me like a rat. By forming a chain gang my parents managed to drag me to the safety of the next carriage and thereafter we did not complain about the heat.

Norway was magnificent! Looking through my steaming window I could see our locomotive burrowing into the heart of a mountain like some precocious mole. Minutes of darkness followed while we followed the great mole trek, and then, by looking back I could see our tail returning from the underworld.

That railway system was inspired, I swear, by Pluto – the Disney character as much as the Greek god. I lost count of the tunnels bored between Bergen and Oslo. Anyone who travels in Norway and fails to believe in trolls and giants is insensitive indeed. The enchanted scene gives credence to the fairyland of Hans Andersen and Edward Grieg.

Across the white Hardanger Fjeld we rattled, stopping at stations so snowed-in that passengers had to climb upwards from the train. The whole journey took fourteen hours and the lights of Oslo, reflected in a wood-girt fjord, made a welcome sight. Less welcome was the appearance of the emissary who met us at the station.

His name, translated from Norwegian, was Dear Wolf. A black wide-brimmed hat shaded a cadaverous countenance and a black coat draped his thin, lithe frame. He appeared to have stepped straight from the text of a who-dun-it, but whether or not he packed a gun would have been impolite to ask.

'You vill kom vis me,' he intoned sombrely. 'Your programme is arranged and everytink is vaiting.'

We never discovered the exact nature of his profession, but he seemed to pull a lot of weight in diplomatic circles. He apparently knew everybody, and the merest waggle of his little finger brought people running. Before Father's first public concert in the great Aula Hall, Dear Wolf gave my parents a thorough briefing.

'Kink Haakon is koming,' he said, 'and ven the kink has valked down the izal to his seat, you Messter Vite, will mount your pulpit and conduct the National Anthems of our countries.

'You, Meesis Vite, vill vear your lonk blue dress and not so much jewels as you might think. The boy [that was me] vil vear his most pretty suit and shirt. . . .'

He had the whole thing planned and timed to the second like a grand bank robbery. But for all his major-domo efficiency and dictorial manner I began to warm to the man. He and I shared a common interest in wildlife and fishing.

'Ven ve go fishink in Norvay,' he told me, 've travel on a horse vith all our food. End ve never forget to take our booter-bokas.' This last had me stumped, and I showed my puzzlement.

'Booter,' he explained, ' – the stuff you use for spreading on your brod. Ve alvays carry it in a leetle bokas.'

His English was at least better than my Norwegian and I soon discovered that if I spoke in the broadest Aberdeen accent I could muster I could make myself better understood. A phrase like 'bairns gaun to the squeal' (children going to school) was readily understood. Norway and my native county, it seemed, had many words in common, and even the lilting cadences of intonation were similar. Mother was horrified to hear me blethering like a Donside orraman, and failed to grasp the point that I was improving communications.

Even Father, rehearsing the orchestra, took a leaf from my book. Telling the brass section that they were behind the beat had no effect. The offenders simply gave him a blank look. Squatting down he began to belabour his own bottom, shouting 'Behind . . . efter . . . your airse . . .' and the grinning musicians got the message at once.

On the morning after the concert, while bullfinches, common as sparrows in Oslo, and red squirrels gladdened the trees outside our hotel, Dear Wolf came loping into my parents' room.

'You are invited to take lunch vith the kink,' he announced gravely. And there followed the customary briefing, this time on the dos and don'ts of meeting Norwegian royalty.

'You vill enter the kink's presence first, Meester Vite, then Meesis Vite and the boy. The mens vill bow from the vaist up, and Meesis Vite vill make her leetle bob. . . .'

The thought of making a clumsy, awkward entrance filled me with dread and I was in something of a twitter when we reached the palace. A broad staircase swept grandly upwards and at the top stood Crown Prince Olaf (later the king). Hauling myself up by the bannister meant having to walk, not on the stair carpet, but on the shining white surround. I was red with embarrassment.

Prince Olaf conducted us to his father, King Haakon, an immensely tall, thin man exuding a warmth that would have melted a glacier. Father bowed and mother curtsied – so suddenly in front of me that I, in bowing, stumbled over her and only regained balance by leaning on her back.

'Ah, Mr Whyte,' the king was saying, 'how good it is to see you, and how much I enjoyed your concert. All my life I have wanted to be a conductor.'

To my horror, Father responded: 'How kind, sir – all my life I have wanted to be a king.'

For an instant the world stopped turning, and then, there was great Haakon laughing uproariously at Father's ice-breaker, and slapping him on the shoulder and patting my mother, and squeezing my hand in his great warm paw. Lunch went like a dream. A band played Scottish and Norwegian music below our window, and we talked of shoes, ships, sealing wax and candlesticks. Kings, as I recall, were not mentioned again.

Dear Wolf, when told of Father's opening *bon mot*, shook his gloomy head. 'Your father is a very naughty man,' he said. 'I must find vays of trimming him to fit.'

He seized his opportunity at a dinner held for Father by officials of the British Embassy. He had composed a highly amusing speech in his inimitable, if unidiomatic, English, but fortunately I was at his side to save him from making a fearful gaffe.

'I am right, am I not,' he whispered, 'in referring to your father as "the black bastard of the family"?'

'Sheep,' I hissed at him.

'Ah,' said Dear Wolf, "the black bastard sheep of the family".'

'The black sheep of the family,' I corrected.

ing on the Lake of Menteith, 1976

Three weeks old and in my mother's arms (with Airedale, Winnie) in the garden of Millbank, Aboyne

With my father

'That first Leviathan', with the old Daimler in the background

On my first picnic after polio, being encouraged by friends

Right: My wife Anne pictured after polio

Below: Cub reporter, 1951

Far right: My father, Ian Whyte

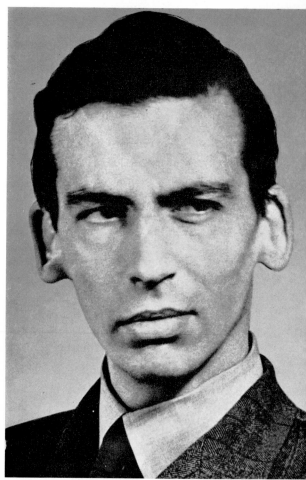

Right: Mr Sim, 'the first philosopher', in Tomintoul with his 'white heather' beard

Below: At helm of yacht *Owl* in Atlantic, west of the Isle of Mull, 1962

h Ross Kennedy (left) leaving Queen's Dock, Glasgow, aboard *Mairi* en route
Ardnamurchan

Owl's dinghy (right), being rowed astern into Fingal's Cave, Isle of Staffa

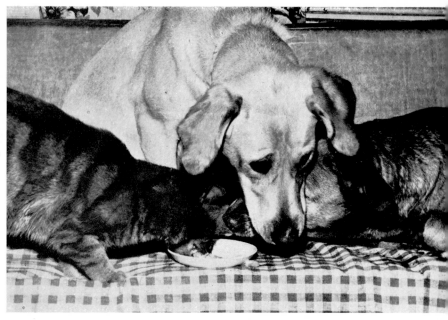

Cambus (centre) is introduced to our cat and to Brandy for the first time

My first attempt at canoeing on Loch Lomond

'But you have a nursery rhyme,' he insisted, 'about black bastard sheep having any vool.'

'Baa, baa black sheep,' I said, raising my voice, and our nearest neighbours, who had overheard most of the conversation were in stitches.

Dear Wolf kept pressing me to wine, and its unaccustomed bouquet swam to my head. Almost to my own astonishment – and certainly to my parents' – I found myself on my feet making a speech of my own. I cannot recall a word of it; but seemingly it extolled the virtues and kinship of Scotland and Norway. It was the first speech I made in public and, for a long enough time, the last. At least it was graciously received by my elders.

At the end of a week Dear Wolf, looking more like a spy than ever, came to see us off on the ship bound for Newcastle. He came bearing gifts. For Father there was a bottle of Aquavit, for Mother a present of chocolate 'eclaikers' and for me – a booter-bokas. I was sorry to see the last of my mysterious friend.

A full gale followed us across the North Sea and on the first night out our ship became alive with a myriad non-paying passengers. Spring was on the way and the gusty air was full of migrants, will-o'-the-wisp creatures of the storm. All night a hen chaffinch sat on the handle of my cabin door. She would sidle fearlessly on to my finger but refused all offerings of food. The great annual call to cross 500 miles of ocean had taken grip of her and her kind, and for a while had removed all terror of mankind.

By morning the ship's lifeboats were roosts for blackbirds and starlings, assured by some divine faith that they were travelling in the right direction. Less certain was a worried oyster-catcher who made the foremast his perch and every half hour or so would rise and circle the ship to ascertain that she was on the right course. Borne by the spray-drenched wind, flocks of buntings passed our bows in dipping, dripping flight, brushing the manes of the white sea stallions, bound for the dim certainty of a distant shore.

Never in all my hours at sea have I been more enthralled. To be sailing home is always wonderful; but to bring spring along, visible and even tangible, is manna for the soul. By the time we had docked in Newcastle not a bird remained aboard: they were already far inland, rediscovering the fields and woodlands of their birth.

Home again in Glasgow, thoughts of university began to loom large. Glasgow University had accepted my entry in principle, but admission depended on my gaining a pass in a higher Latin entrance exam. I got through by the skin of my teeth. And now, to facilitate journeys between home and university I began to pester my father to buy a car. I had already learned to drive a van while at Dollar, propping up my right leg on a log of wood in order to reach the brake pedal – dangerous but highly instructive. Now, armed with a provisional licence, I desperately wanted a car of my own.

Father grumbled about the expense. In the years immediately following the war cars were costly and hard to come by. But at last he bought a second-hand Riley Nine for £350 – more than its price when new in 1933. KV 6488 was a real enthusiast's car, a near vintage banger with a crash gearbox. The least mistiming of any gear resulted in an agony of gnashing teeth, ivory as well as metal. Every little illness of the engine demanded the patience of a surgeon and the attentiveness of a nurse. But how I loved that little red tyrant! At last I was mobile beyond dreams, and in my gratitude I learned to cherish every nut and bolt.

Hit more in his pocket than by my new-found freedom, Father suggested that I might do something to defray expenses.

'Why don't you try writing something for BBC Children's Hour?' he suggested. 'Kathleen Garscadden is always looking for new material. Anything that is accepted will always earn you some petrol money.'

I kept putting off the evil moment. Anything I wrote, I thought, would never make the grade. Children's Hour was for children, and here was I grappling with the business of growing up. Many of my friends had shot down planes and travelled a man's world. Fairy tales and 'once up a times' would make me a laughing stock among them. I had not the wit to see that my service-minded, extrovert contemporaries wanted nothing so much as an escape from reality.

Father tackled me once again. 'Just sit down and write,' he ordered. He did not often order, and when he did I obeyed.

I had fiddled around with verses about a cat, that most felicitous of animals, and now I began to expand on the theme:

> There was a cat whose name is Bran
> Wha fears nor beast, nor ghaist, nor man
> And prowls around the countryside
> From Inverness to East Kilbride
> And back again . . .

Bran's first adventure ran to about eleven minutes and I submitted it to Kathleen, who was head of Children's Hour programmes in Scotland. To my amazement she liked it – and asked if I could produce a whole series, one every fortnight.

Bran was a sort of anti-hero, a kind of cuddly character who pretended to be tremendously brave while all the time hiding a faint heart behind bristling whiskers. He dressed in the most outlandish clothes, had a wife and son, and lived in the fiction village of Gaberlonie. He was essentially Scottish in character, and quite naturally shared my delight in atrocious puns. Every now and again he would compose a nonsense poem:

> Once there was a sealion, a slithery sleekit sealion
> Wha spent his time reclining in the surf beside the sea;
> And as he was a-lyin' by the sea he used to think
> That a sealion was the nicest kind of animile to be.
>
> And there also was a limpet – an awfu' skimpit limpet –
> Wha had one foot and limpit on a crutch along the sand.
> And since he didna like being lame he simply had to lump it
> – Which was hard upon the limpet, as I'm sure you'll understand.
>
> One day the limpet made a bee-line for to go and see the sealion
> Wha was lyin' in the surf beside the sea as I have said.
> The limpet limpit up and asked the sealion, maist politely,
> 'Is a sealion just a feline or a kind of seal instead?'
> But the sealion didna like being asked, and so he ate the limpet
> Which didna satisfy the limpet's curiosity.
> But it satisfied the sealion wha by now was feelin' fine;
> For it doesn't really matter to a satisfied sealion
> As to whether he's a sealion or a seal or else a feline
> So long as, after dining, he's left alone, reclining,
> Digesting skimpit limpets in the surf beside the sea.

Burning inside me all the while was the desire to write music. Father did not exactly dissuade me, but he was insistent that I should master the discipline and techniques of the art in which he himself was so proficient. I must learn to read and write music proficiently without recourse to the piano, hearing chords and counterpoints inside my head. But I was never able to acquire the necessary facility.

Father, with his back turned, could infallibly identify a randon handful of notes played on the keyboard. He could read the full score of a symphony as easily as most people scan a newspaper.

Practice, he claimed, was the only recipe for success – and practice, goodness knows, had occupied most of the waking hours of his lifetime. But he seemed to discount his own phenomenal talent, that indefinable natural ability which makes practice easy and genius possible. Genius, he was fond of quoting, is one per cent inspiration and ninety-nine per cent perspiration; but I think Edison's definition falls short of the truth. It works perhaps for the musician who aspires to creating great music, or for the scientist who seeks to prove an advanced theory. But I doubt if Edison's formula would have helped Einstein to write the B Minor Mass, or Bach to discover the theory of relativity.

Composition, I found, was a painful business. I knew what I wanted to say, the effect I wanted to produce, but lacked the ability to make myself articulate. I would spend hours strumming at the piano with a pencil clamped between my teeth, ready to jot down chords before they became irretrievably lost. Progress was frustratingly slow. Father viewed my efforts with a kind tolerant scepticism. While he was not slow to encourage me in other directions, he seemed reluctant to have me following in his footsteps. Perhaps he realized that I could never match his length of stride.

I managed, however, to complete a short piece – a serenade for solo violin and small orchestra – and showed it to Kemlo Stephen who was then conductor of the BBC Scottish Variety Orchestra. I was astounded when he invited me to conduct its performance at a forthcoming broadcast. With a casual air which scarcely concealed my excitement I mentioned the matter to Father. He did not, it struck me at the time, seem particularly interested.

My nerves jangled like a shattered harp as I took the rehearsal. During the first run through I had to correct one or two wrong notes, apologizing for the errors to the patient professional musicians in front of me. When everything was shipshape I decided to have a final trial.

The solo violin soared, oboe, clarinet and bassoon merged sweetly with the rest of the strings. But from the piano, its raised lid hiding the player, there issued the most dreadful din imaginable. I had not the vaguest idea what had gone wrong, or how to correct it. Sweating with terror, I asked if we might play the offending passage again.

But the ensuing noise was worse than before. The orchestra giggled and tittered and my face was burning with shame and embarrassment. How I longed for some cool hole to open in the floor below me. I was debating whether to flee the scene or face up to the situation when the pianist revealed himself. Never before, I think, has son been so relieved to welcome father.

By substituting himself as pianist he had been able to keep an unobtrusive paternal eye on proceedings. But it offered him still another opportunity to play one of his musical jokes. As he walked out of the studio he stopped and gave the orchestra and myself a knowing smile.

'I don't think my services are really required,' he said. The broadcast which followed was completely successful. But any illusions I may have had about being an aspiring conductor-composer dispersed like morning mists.

Music, I realized – had possibly always realized – was too precarious a profession for a limited talent like mine. Painting appealed to me, as did writing poetry, but the stories I had heard about artists existing in gusty garrets, utterly devoted to the muse of their choice, influenced me to choose some career less fickle.

It was not that I wanted to make a lot of money. In fact, I rather despised those who did. I did not like fat, cigar-shaped men with gilt-edged brains who induced pound notes to breed with the unseemly frequency of mice. One could sometimes assess their humanity by examining their bookcases. The Bible, Shakespeare, Dickens, Scott and Shaw had the habit of standing stiffly to attention on their shelves, pages unsullied by loving inspection – and often even uncut. I had the makings of an intellectual snob. Had I had the full use of my limbs I think I would have taken up some rural calling – gamekeeping or forestry perhaps – and augmented my earnings by writing and illustrating nature books.

Father's immediate idea was that I should become a parish minister or, failing that, the keeper of a country inn – a sort of choice between the sublime and the bibulous. I felt that I was too great a sinner to become the former and too much of an idealist for the latter.

Mother was adamant that I continue at university and take my degree. What profession I chose did not matter. A degree was all that counted. I know that she had my best interests at heart, but she left me with the impression that a lavatory attendant with an M.A. is preferable to one without. She may have been right: a degree perhaps opens more doors.

For a while I plodded on. My contemporaries at Glasgow University were faced, for the most part, with uncertainties like my own. The majority were ex-Servicemen returning to complete disrupted studies. They were men of the world who had fought and won, who had known privation and the rigours of hard discipline in war. Many of them did not settle easily to the self-discipline of learning.

Their mood and mine accorded pretty well. I admired their swash-buckling ways and their tales of conquest, amatory as well as military. I refought their battles with them, basking somehow in their reflected glory. They must have known how green and immature I was and yet they accepted me in their company. Perhaps they realized how badly I needed to grow up. Somehow I contrived to do a modicum of work.

The cranial nerves of the dogfish, the rumblings of old Descartes (thinking that he was what he was because he thought), the analysis of fugue and appraisals of the meta-physical poets all rubbed some of their pollen off in my mind. Bran the Cat continued to have incredible adventures on Children's Hour, and some of his devotees, I was surprised to find, were men who had bombed Berlin and suffered ill-treatment in Japanese hands. A chance meeting with a sub-editor on the *Glasgow Herald* gave me the opportunity of doing the occasional book review for his paper: my appraisals of the works of a few contemporary writers was kinder, I think, than that which my English professor bestowed on my Anglo-Saxon translations.

One of my university friends who was a young German named Heinz. He was a fair-haired, sensitive lad who shared my pleasure in poetry and music. It seemed incredible that he, at the age of sixteen, had been hauled into service with the Luftwaffe, had learned to fly a Stuka dive bomber, and had been shot down and captured on his first mission. Everyone liked him – even the former RAF boys who had bitter experience of war over Germany. Heinz and his age group, we knew, had been called on by the Nazis to effect a last ditch stand. He was about as pro-Hitler as Winston Churchill.

And yet, when I took him home one night along with other friends, my father bristled like a terrier. How dare I bring a Nazi to the house? he thundered. Fraternizing with the enemy was not included in his code of ethics. Poor Heinz was mortified, but he understood well enough how prejudice dies hard. It took my other friends to mollify Father. If anyone had cause to hate Germans it was they; they had seen atrocity in action, but now that the war was over it was time to work for peace. And what was a laddie of sixteen to do when dragged into Hitler's war machine – comply with authority, or be shot for treason?

Father did not apologize in so many words. It was a situation in which the word 'sorry' would have fallen awkwardly, like a swear word in Sunday school. He crossed the room to the piano instead.

He began to play Schubert, sweetness flowing from his fingers. Heinz listened like one in a dream. He had not, I imagine, heard such music for quite some time. For a moment or two his eyes and Father's met and glowed, and each understood the other's hurt. Forgiveness twinkled among the semi-quavers.

Many of my fellow students were married and living happily, if scantily, on their university grants. I was deeply envious of their marital status. Any difficulty they had in balancing the budget seemed more than amply compensated by their freedom from frustration. A contented bedroom I believed – and still believe – leaves the road clear for concentrated work.

I had my fair quota of girl friends, proposing marriage to each in turn and jilting them with disgraceful regularity. I was the sort of aspiring Lothario against which every woman's magazine directs its fire. That my wild oats never quite got shaken free from the awn spoke more for the character of the girls concerned than for the chivalry of their pursuer. But the time came when I made up my mind finally to get married.

The fact that my parents' marriage was breaking up accelerated rather than inhibited my intentions. Mother and Father both turned to me to act as mediator in their differences. It was a situation which no arbiter could rectify. I was old enough to offer advice, but young enough to be hurt by the position in which I found myself. Life at home grew steadily more intolerable. I felt that the time was ripe for flying the nest. The last straw followed a quarrel which dragged on into the early hours of morning. My parents promised to waken me for an all important zoology exam. I could blame them no more than myself that we all slept in.

I would not, I said, be returning to university. I would start looking for a job immediately. Mother was bitterly disappointed but saw that I had my mind made up. She prophesied that I would regret my decision for the rest of my life. She lived long enough, I am glad to say, to know that her forecast was happily wrong. I have many regrets left strewn behind me, but leaving university is not one of them.

I was there long enough to acquire a love of learning, to realize that education is not something to be discarded like an old coat upon passing a final examination, to understand that knowledge is infinite.

I now began to look for a job in earnest. It seemed to me that journalism might offer the opportunity I was looking for. But the newspapers and magazines I approached expressed their regret that there were no vacancies. I considered them a short-sighted lot.

I was not to know that the typical journalist became

apprenticed to his trade upon leaving school. His practice ground was usually a local weekly – 'the squeak' as it is so delightfully and affectionately called in Scotland – where he reported such momentous matters as council meetings, church bazaars, bowling dinners and weddings, down to the last details of what the bride's mother was wearing.

I had still to read for myself the superb story written by a cub reporter on the subject of a wedding ceremony in Rutherglen. He had spared no effort in describing every item of interest. He had written to considerable length, had sub-edited his own copy and 'put it to bed'. His effusion ended thus: 'To the accompaniment of music for two violins and a harp, the marriage was consummated at the altar.'

What I did not know was that I was destined to perpetrate a few journalistic horrors of my own – and on a national level at that.

I was finally granted an audience by the late Mr A. C. Trotter – Sandy to his many friends – editor of the *Scottish Daily Express* and one of Scotland's great newspapermen.

I hirpled into his presence with all the courage displayed by a Chihuahua in the territory of a Great Dane. His terse speech and down-right manner betokened the man of action, the maker of swift decisions. He came straight to the point. What, he asked, was my knowledge or experience of newspapers? – I had to confess it was negligible. What then did I have in the way of writing ability? What contribution did I think I might make to a national daily paper?

I spoke of my book reviews, my work for Children's Hour and my liking for the arts. I said I thought I might have the makings of a music critic. I must have sounded about as lame as I looked. Mr Trotter did not look impressed. He talked about life on a newspaper, its long hours, its chores and excitements, its dependence on speed and efficiency. Did I feel that I was equal to the challenge? I said that I felt I was. This was the end of the interview – the most important of my young life. Mr Trotter said he would get in touch with me letting me know if a staff vacancy could be found.

As he showed me from the sanctum I asked a stupid question: 'You will let me know, won't you?'

He gave me the glare that I was to come to know so well

on future occasions. 'I told you I would, didn't I?' he replied.

It wasn't that I doubted his word; it was simply that I was so anxious to know my luck. I went home full of misgivings. I had surely painted a poor picture of myself. I had shown myself as a failed student, a dilettante, a lame duck . . . but two days later a letter arrived. It offered me a position as trainee reporter at a weekly wage of £6. Would I please report to Mr Jack Campbell, News Editor, on the following Monday at 9 a.m.

My joy knew no bounds. A new world stretched before me, unknown, uncharted. For the first time in my life I stood on the threshold of independence.

9

Into Rough Waters

The shining black façade of the *Express* building in Glasgow's Albion Street glittered in the grey light of morning. It was 10 December 1950. The news room three floors above street level was beginning to thrum with activity.

Jack Campbell, the News Editor, was juggling with three separate calls and endeavouring to make notes at the same time. I remember thinking that an octupus would have been better equipped, physically speaking, to handle the situation. When a spare moment presented itself he welcomed me to the fold.

'How's your shorthand?' was his first question. I had to confess that it was not well at all; that, in fact, it did not exist. He advised to start learning fast. Meanwhile he would introduce me to his reporting staff, and they in turn would explain the workings of the editorial department.

They were a jovial lot, men a little older than myself, many of whom had known military service. It soon became apparent to me that there was another war to be won. When orders were snapped out men jumped to obey. Guiding our destiny from his London eyrie was the redoubtable Lord Beaverbrook, a man whose scintillating power and influence was like a physical presence in our midst.

The jargon of my new profession came strangely to my ears. Copy was what we wrote. Filing it meant submitting the finished article. Spiking it was what sub-editors did, because it was rubbish, or because there was no room for it in the paper, or even because their ulcers were hurting.

Jack Coupar was chief reporter, a lean man with shrewd

blue eyes and a mouth set like a rat trap. He had commanded a tank corps during the war and had lost none of his crisp authority. He took me out to lunch and told me what was expected of me. If I thought I could take life easy because I was lame I had better think again. I was going to learn the hard way and he would see to it that I did. No, I would not be asked to climb Ben Nevis or engage in any dangerous work: there were fit men enough in the office to cope with hazardous assignments. But I would do my fair share of covering murders, fires, street accidents, court cases, disputes and disasters.

My stomach seemed to be tied in a granny knot and my food lay untouched on my plate.

That afternoon I was given my first assignment. There had been a court case, a man convicted of assault, and the *Express* deemed it necessary to grace its Scottish editions with a photograph of the gentleman concerned. Would I go and collect a photograph of him?

The address, indelibly etched on my mind, was 110 Parliamentary Road. The house was on the top floor of a grim tenement. To reach it I had to press hands against filthy walls to lever myself up four flights of stairs (there was no handrail). Panting, I arrived at my destination and knocked on the door.

I had already rehearsed a polite little speech: 'I'm from the *Daily Express*. I wonder if you'd be kind enough to let me borrow a photograph of Mr – ' but the words were never uttered.

The door burst open. A huge man wearing braces over a hairy vest stood there brandishing a bottle of gin. He roared some fearful obscenity, raised the bottle and lurched towards me.

My instinct was to turn and run, but I knew if I turned my back I was lost. I stepped forward instead. 'I wouldn't if I were you,' I said. 'The police are downstairs and I've only got to give them a shout. . . .'

What divine providence prompted me to tell that lie I will never know. To my amazement it stopped him in his tracks. He retreated, mumbling, and closed the door. Quivering like a blancmange and trying to stifle sobs of terror, I slithered down those hellish stairs, dreading the sound of following footsteps.

Back at the office I buttonholed Jack Campbell. 'Did you get the picture?' he asked.

'I did not,' I bleated. 'I am sorry to say that I have to hand in my resignation. I cannot and will not tolerate being threatened by drunken thugs.'

He got the whole story out of me bit by bit and roared with laughter. 'Forget it,' he said. 'Go down to the pub and have a drink.'

Sent one day to cover a conscientious objectors' tribunal, I listened to the evidence along with other pressmen and was rather puzzled when the chairman of the tribunal asked us to leave the room. I returned to Albion Street to be asked the result of the hearing. 'There was none forthcoming,' I said. 'We were told to go away.'

'My God,' said Jack Campbell, 'you only leave the room while the tribunal considers the evidence. They call you back in when they've reached a verdict.'

My early days as a reporter were sheer agony. At home at night I had to pretend to my parents that all was well. I dared not let them know that I thought my choice of career was the biggest error I had ever made. I had to grin and endure.

Every morning the editor posted a notice in the news room praising, or finding fault with, the stories which appeared in the paper. My name never appeared on the honours list, nor even among the annals of the damned. It was little wonder, for my copy seldom escaped the dreaded spike.

But my chance came one day when I was the only reporter around when someone telephoned to say that a mad bullock had escaped from Glasgow's cattle market.

'Will I take a photographer?' I asked the News Editor hopefully. I could see him searching the room frantically for the sight of a fit man, but none appeared. The job was mine.

I ordered a car, collected a photographer and set off towards the market. The disruption to civic peace was easy to spot. A crowd of several hundred children ran whooping along Duke Street in pursuit of the bullock, which, if not utterly mad, was certainly not well pleased. The chase had a distinctly Spanish flavour and led us to waste ground near Alexandra Parade.

It was there that the ugly black brute singled me out for special attention, lowered his handlebars, pawed the ground and charged. I tried to climb a drainpipe but got my caliper jammed between it and the wall. My exit from this world seemed imminent when a gallant policeman diverted my assailant's attention by seizing hold of its tail. The bullock's final capture and the chaos he had created in Glasgow's east end made good material for copy. Next morning I had the satisfaction of seeing my name on the honours list.

Journalism, I discovered, had also its harrowing moments. One Sunday morning when people happier than I were snug in bed or church, I found myself toiling up tenement stairs (nothing ever happened to folk at ground level) to interview a young woman whose husband had been killed in a fall from a crane.

When she answered the door I was relieved to see that she seemed quite composed, strangely cheerful in fact. When I told her that I represented a newspaper a shadow crossed her face. Was something wrong, she asked?

Horrified, I realized that she had not yet been told of the accident. I asked if I might come in, got her to sit down and broke the news as gently and firmly as I could. She did not flinch or weep. She simply stared at me.

'You poor soul,' she said. 'You've climbed all those stairs to tell me my man's dead . . . I'll just go and make you a cup of tea.'

I had never met such selflessness before. It was not as if she had not loved her husband. She sat and spoke to me about him, telling me about their happy times together, caressing his name with soft speech. But how kind I had been to come and tell her, to break the news gently. Perhaps the tears would come later, welling into the loneliness of her pillow; but for the moment – maybe for all time – her courage burned like a cold flame. She shamed me to the roots of my being.

Office hours and desk work, I began to find, had little appeal. I had no ambition, unlike most of my colleagues, to jostle for position on the rungs of the paper ladder. If I envied the men at the top at all it was because their pay packets were fatter than mine. But their hair was usually greyer, their faces paler and their stomachs more dyspeptic. Money, I was able to agree with Professor Joad, does not bring happiness: it merely enables you to be miserable in greater comfort. Having too much of the stuff is probably worse for the health than having too little.

Our office windows looked out on Blackfriars Church (now razed for ever from the Glasgow scene) and on the kirk steps on fine days in summer an old ragged couple would rendezvous, he with his bottle of cheap port, and she with her half-bottle of methylated spirits. They sat on God's steps, swigging their fire water until something akin to happiness blazed on their furrowed faces. They laughed and cackled and cuddled. Incredibly, on one occasion, they started the preliminaries to making love, cheered on by our vanmen in the street below while the swifts screamed overhead. Ugly as their wrinkled passion seemed, there was something pathetic and childlike about them. Unlike the sickle-winged birds above them they were thralled to the city. Unlike the birds they had no real freedom. When the police van arrived to take them away the men in the street booed and jeered, perhaps because they had been denied some vicarious entertainment, but also, I think, because they recognized in those ancient sweethearts the longing to be free from the shackles of society.

Dogs may mate in the street, and human beings may not. It would be an appalling state of affairs if custom and taste decreed otherwise. But what artificial creatures we have become, so wrapped in thicknesses of law, religion, habit and superstition that we scarcely recognize our biological selves!

Stuck in an office in the grey, hammering heart of a city, I found myself longing again for the broad horizons of the countryside. Like Yeats I could always hear lake waters lapping. Those who thought that my infirmity made me the ideal candidate to sit chained to a desk had little notion of the truth; in the office I always felt something of a prisoner.

When jobs cropped up out of town I was never happier.

One such assignment came my way when the German sail training schooner *Gorch Fock* paid a goodwill visit to Aberdeen. I did not dream that her coming would lead me, indirectly, into rougher waters than I had imagined possible.

The schooner was due to berth in Aberdeen harbour early one autumn morning. The News Desk, whose experience seemed to derive from *Treasure Island*, wanted pictures of her sweeping into harbour under full sail (had she done so, she would have knocked a grievous dent in the granite city). They wanted shots of cadets strung along the yard-arms like swallows on a wire. They wanted salty words from me full of 'Avast there, me hearties' and 'Down with the stays'l' or their German equivalents. More than anything they wanted a picture-story to boost circulation in the area.

The sun was up and glittering on Aberdeen Bay as I reached the heights above Stonehaven and there, heading inshore as if to make harbour ahead of schedule, was the training ship. I fairly hurtled the last dozen miles to Aberdeen, banged on the office door and frightened half the pigeons in Belmont Street. My panic was needless. The *Gorch Fock* was biding her time, tacking again to seaward before making her grand entrance.

Photographer Ron Taylor and I stood at the harbour discussing strategy. We quickly agreed that, if good pictures were to be taken of the ship, we would have to put to sea ourselves. We decided to charter a pilot cutter. While local pressmen hung around dreaming of bulging canvas, or perhaps, in fairness, content to photograph the ship under bare poles, we quietly slipped out from harbour. Clearing the mole, we scanned the sea and saw, to our dismay, that the *Gorch Fock* was a mere speck on the horizon. It was cold and choppy when we finally caught up with her six miles out in the North Sea, but the sight of her lives with us yet.

As we came under her heeling hull we looked up into the vast, orderly jungle of her rigging. Her full press of sail thundered in the breeze, and even above the great roar of sail, the sound of the wind in her shrouds and halyards rang like an orchestra of harps. Ah, here was freedom and music beyond most men's dreams! But as we were soon to learn, this was the freedom born of strict discipline.

A dog barked. Ron and I stared at each other: like drunks we required the reassurance of 'yes, I hear it too'; for dogs, in our experience were rare in the North Sea. But there, sure enough, was a fox terrier yapping his whiskers off at us from the schooner's poop.

As we followed her in, the ship's crew began to furl sail, giddying 100 feet above us. Ron lay on his back in our rolling boat, clicking his shutter, savouring every second. We lurched happily ashore and tried to look modest as we passed a throng of waiting rivals. I think, however, they already knew that somewhere along the line they had missed out.

I do not know if the captain of the *Gorch Fock* was asked to put back to sea, or even hoist sail in harbour. In any event he did not. What I do remember is how German crewmen queued up the following day to buy copies of our newspaper by the half-dozen.

Der Herr Kapitän was himself delighted. He threw *eine kleine* party and invited us pressmen along. I have never seen a ship in such immaculate trim. Her brasswork was polished mirror bright. Years of scrubbing had made her decks as spotless as a dress shirt. Ropes and sheets lay coiled as neat as onion rings. As we went aboard, her cadets stood so stiffly to attention that they seemed to have been starched in position. Heels clicked like cap pistols and arms snapped to the salute. As we were escorted to the captain's quarters I had the ridiculous feeling that I should be doing the goose-step. Our host bristled with gold braid and geniality, bade us all be seated, and left us in no doubt that we were as welcome as dancing girls in Barlinnie Prison.

Stewards marched in with trays of drinks and savouries. The instant a glass was emptied it was replenished. My own personal attendant stood at my elbow anticipating my every wish, however trivial. When I reached for a cigarette he thrust a silver box before me. When I wanted to flick, an ashtray was whisked within reach and returned to its exact place on the table. At one juncture I hesitated before scratching my ear in case my robot had been programmed to do it for me.

As this impressive party progressed, the captain's joviality fairly bubbled. I felt that the appearance and running of his ship was to be complimented, and told him so. I also mentioned my surprise at having been barked at in mid ocean by a real sea dog.

'Aha!' he roared. 'So you have realized the truth about my ship. I am not the captain here. My dog is the master. Bring in the dog!'

Heels snapped, and within seconds the real captain was snuffling in our midst. With all the panache of a prize-winning dowager at Cruft's, mine host went into raptures over his dog's pedigree, the length of which was well in excess of its temper.

'You know all about discipline, don't you, dog?' his owner cried. 'Go and bite the mate!'

The first officer stood stiffly to attention. In a snarling frenzy the terrier launched himself at his starboard ankle and began to worry it. I think we all expected the mate to execute a jig, to kick the dog aside – at least to react. But he did not. He stood stiff and unflinching, his eyes staring unwinkingly ahead of him, his expression registering neither pain nor amusement.

The owner heaved with merriment. 'Now you see who is master of the ship – hey?'

All too plainly we saw. Nobody joined in the laughter. There came the sudden murmur of everyone trying to change the subject. It only served to break up the party.

It is perhaps not strange that when you have some success with a yarn, you are expected, sooner or later, to give an encore. I was barely ashore when Adam Borthwick, our head man in the north, mentioned that the Isle of Islay was due to receive a new lifeboat in a few days' time. Eagerly I snatched at another chance to avoid office tedium, and the News Desk raised no objections. And neither did one Commander Wicksteed, in charge of the northern area of the RNLI. Since that institution depends on public subscription, some publicity would be welcome.

'Join us at Portpatrick,' he invited. 'You'll have to come down the night before we sail for Islay as we intend leaving at first light.'

I should have told him, I suppose, that his intending passenger was rather lame on the hoof, but I held my tongue.

He might just have turned me down. Some of my friends shook sad heads: they had had encounters with lifeboats before. Even in a slight sea, they said, these vessels wallow like pigs: I would require a supply of little paper bags and a modicum of the wine of the country in my luggage. There were easier ways to die, they said. And if their jibes made me feel a trifle uneasy, the feeling was amplified by the state of the weather. Stilettos of rain had begun to slash at the windows. The chimney cowls of tenements were spinning in rattling pirouette. There was that giddy, heady feeling in the air when you know the barometer is dropping fast.

Reg Lancaster was the photographer detailed to accompany me. If he guessed what lay in store for us he said nary a word to me. At 9 p.m. on a raving November night we left by car for Portpatrick 100 miles away.

Portpatrick Hotel, I would almost swear, was rocking on its cliff-top when we arrived. Prising open the car doors was a feat of strength; and that once achieved, preventing them being torn from their hinges was another. We fluttered into the hotel like autumn leaves, and drifted to rest against the bar counter.

The lifeboat's crew was preparing for an early night. The men were not saying very much, and what they did have to impart was not reassuring. They had sailed that morning from Donaghadee in Ireland. The harbourmaster had suggested that they stay put, but their commander, Vice-Admiral Wyndham Quinn (RN retd) had decreed otherwise. On passing Donaghadee Light on the way out they were lifted on the crest of a freak wave. This enabled them to look horizontally at the top of the light, some sixty feet above the sea, and the experience had not filled their hearts with joy, and hearing it recounted evoked no merriment in mine, which was beating a Bossa Nova down about my boots. Anyway, we would have to be at the harbour before 6 a.m., ready to board. It was now midnight, and unexpectedly I was called to the telephone.

My surprise at hearing Sandy Trotter's voice was considerable. Personal calls from the editor to juniors were rare indeed, and I could hear concern in his tone.

'The weather forecast is very bad,' he said. 'You don't

have to go on that boat if you don't want to. Just forget the whole thing.'

Here at last was the excuse to quit – provided, no less, by the Old Man himself. Here was the chance to sleep with all wild fears stilled. But no: there is a fear worse than fear itself, and that is the dread of being thought afraid. If that boat sailed out into the storm without me, I would wonder for the rest of my days what I had missed by not being there. I would never know my own limits or those of my companions, and this would haunt me like a chronic pain. All this swept through my mind in an instant without actually being thought out, and I knew I was too great a coward to give up now.

As if my voice belonged to someone else, I heard it saying: 'There's a chance that the wind may moderate before morning. I'd like to make the trip. Would you leave me to make the final decision before the boat sails?'

'Well, it's your stomach,' said Sandy Trotter, 'but don't do anything daft.'

I hung up and cursed my other self for being all the idiots this side of Islay. Reg probably thought we were mad too, but gave that shy grin of his and said: 'I'm not a very good sailor but let's try it.'

I stood at my bedroom window and looked out through glass which seemed to bend in the gale. By the lights of the hotel I could see drove after drove of white sea stallions being herded ashore from rough pastures. I lay in bed and listened to their hooves thundering on rock. Somehow I managed to doze until dawn.

We all foregathered at the harbour, staggering in the wind like a skein of geese. I had to cling to a stanchion to keep myself from falling, and I think it was about then that Vice-Admiral Wyndham Quinn realized he had a lame duck among his brood. He was a man in his sixties, tall, hawk-eyed and glistening in his oilskins.

'I can't sail with a disabled man,' he said brusquely. 'On whose authority are you here?'

I told him. But Commander Wicksteed had not yet arrived. When he finally showed up, the pair of them started a fairly strenuous argument over what was to be done with my body.

The prospect of putting to sea in such a storm seemed bad enough without the added misery of being unloved and unwanted. It was Wicksteed who finally clinched the matter.

'I agreed to take you, and take you I will,' he said. 'If everyone will kindly get aboard, we will now prepare to sail.'

So this was it, the final commitment, no U-turns now. I was hoisted aboard the lifeboat and given the casualty berth. Canvas webbing was strapped between my legs and clipped to a bulkhead. I felt rather embarrassed to be sitting there like a chicken on a spit, but I soon had reason to be grateful. No sooner had we cleared the harbour than the sea smote us. Skulls cracked against bulkheads and arms flailed the air searching for any hand-hold available. At least my canvas harness offered some security.

The wind was roughly north, blowing Force 8 and gusting up to Force 9. After the first moments of stunned shock I was able to take some notice of our vessel's behaviour in a big sea. She would climb up the side of an oncoming wave, hang teetering for a moment, and then plunge with a sickening crunch into the trough beyond. The next wave she would try to bore through while a cold, green deluge cascaded through her half-open cockpit into our cabin below. As she lunged and corkscrewed northwards the needle of her roll-counter swung as far as seventy-eight degrees to either side. A bucking bronco is possibly more uncomfortable to ride but the buster has to sit in the saddle for only a few seconds. We had nine and a half hours ahead of us. Poor Reg, who had turned a delicate shade of eau-de-nil, left the cabin and lay out in the open in the boat's after well. Someone heaped a pile of oilies on top of him, but I think he was too ill to care. My own nausea was due not to sea sickness but to the curse of a vivid imagination.

We sat with our feet on biscuit tins while the sea surged in and out of our scuppers, and when someone suggested brewing up tea all eyes turned hopefully to me. Although she had cost some £40 000 to build, the new lifeboat was then sadly lacking in home comforts. Her paraffin stove was not on gimbals, so that trying to boil water became a prestigious feat. When she rolled to port I had to tilt the pot to starboard, and vice versa, to prevent spillage. Mine were the only hands not busily clinging to supports, but while I dangled in my harness the water took forty-five minutes to boil. Pouring tea into proffered cups was nearly impossible: teapot spout and cup were never in proximity for long enough.

'We'll have hard-boiled eggs instead,' somebody suggested. 'That's the best thing to stop sea sickness.'

The very idea made my stomach waltz: someone else would have to be cook. When at last the eggs were ready I was coaxed into eating one. The taste was vile, but the soothing effect on the tummy was quite remarkable.

All the way out of Portpatrick the distant Kintyre peninsula had afforded us something of a lee, but as we rounded the black cliffs of the Mull we ran into the bared fangs of wind against tide. The waves pitched up into vicious peaks, thirty feet from crest to trough. The gale was now about Force 9 and gusting up to Storm Force 10, sheeting the sea with foam and screaming through our wires like some demented harridan. And now our plunges from wave summit to abyss became a bone-jarring sequence of smashes which seemed destined to break the lifeboat's back; but always she corkscrewed onwards, durable beyond belief, buoyant as a gull. Hanging on was becoming painful and exhausting when the strains of a Gaelic air came ringing out above the storm noise and the drumming of our engines. The singer was John Cameron, a hard bronzed man with clear blue eyes. For the past few hours he had said very little; for in our stormgirt, pitching cabin conversation was virtually impossible. And now his voice rose above the turmoil, hurling a song in praise of his native Islay into the throat of adversity.

'O, my island, O my isle, O my dear, my native soil. . . .' Suddenly we were all singing in a kind of wild ecstasy. We began to feel vividly alive again, and even vaguely triumphant. Wave by wave we were conquering the sea; and haven, still three hours ahead, blossomed out of hope into promise, and from promise into certainty.

'I wish we'd a dram on board,' John shouted. 'But there's no bloody pub out here.'

'I've got a half-bottle in my grip,' I cried. 'But it's stowed away in the for'ard locker.'

John struggled into yellow oilskins, left the cabin and began to crawl along the lurching deck. Three times he fought his way to within feet of his goal, and three times the sea smashed him back in a welter of arms and legs. Had human life been at stake I think he would have kept on trying, but no dram in the world was worth such risk. Until we were well into the lee of Jura my whisky mocked at our misery. When John finally captured it, and bore it in triumph among us, the bottle sped from mouth to mouth and was stone dead inside two minutes. And then, out of the grey sea veils ahead of us, the little whitewashed cottages of Port Askaig stood smiling shyly in the rain. Half of Islay seemed to have gathered on the pier in welcome. Anxious eyes looked down at us. Ready hands made fast our lines and hoisted us ashore. It was then that I began to realize the faith and store which an island people puts in its rescue craft.

For hours they had stared into the storm, straining for a glimpse of us, knowing that their destiny and ours lay in the safe arrival of one small vessel. And now I found myself with arms around the necks of strangers, too numbed with pain to laugh and too happy to cry. I could not walk on the sweet, hard ground. I remember being armed into the bar of the little hotel where warmth and welcome waited. I remember clinging to a chair while the room rolled and plunged around me, and it was days before I regained my land legs. I fell into a deep armchair to sleep the sleep of utter exhaustion – and missed the dinner and speeches in honour of the lifeboat crew.

Nobody seemed to mind. Even the redoubtable Wyndham Quinn unbent a little and 'thought I'd endured the hammering pretty well'. The rabid storm died in the night and the morning sun blazed on a flat blue sea. Back to the lifeboat we trooped for trials in the sound of Islay, and comedy now took a hand in the proceedings.

It had been arranged that, when we fired the rocket line ashore, workers at the local distillery were to make it fast. Our aim, alas, was too good. A sizzling rocket, trailing miles of spiralling rope, crashed into the distillery roof. Shouts of alarm sounded from the shore, but the horrid vision of gallons of precious spirit exploding did not materialize.

Commander Wicksteed, somewhat red-necked, suggested that mention of the incident in a newspaper might not exactly delight officialdom. I promised to keep mum, but our commander had another party trick to do. When we had cut loose from the distillery he produced a long white cylinder from a locker.

'This,' he instructed, 'is a new type of flare. You hold it horizontally. You pull the fuse like this . . . and point the cylinder upwards . . .'

The flare began to go up – and so too did Commander Wicksteed. John Cameron leaned forward, grasped the tail of his jacket and held him down. A great ball of green fire sailed into the blue sky, descended and burst over a herd of deer grazing peacefully on Jura. I have seldom seen animals shift so quickly. Wicksteed, when we looked at him, bore a passable resemblance to Al Jolson, all exposed parts of him being a fairly even black.

'Remember,' he said, 'that it will be heavy weather when you fire this flare. Wind and sea will ensure that you are not burned.'

His crew grinned and John Cameron grinned. Our little commander had a lot of guts.

When, nine years later, John and I met for the last time on his lovely island, we relived every moment of our few fleeting hours together. In our lifetime we spent only three days in each other's company, but three years could not, I think, have drawn us closer. We did not discuss religion or philosophy, or probe each other's minds with the clumsy tools of words. We did not talk about John's wartime exploits when thrice he was torpedoed and thrice navigated his men to safety in open lifeboats over a total distance of 2000 miles, achievements which earned him the OBE and MBE. Not once did he mention the painful illness which was to cut short his days, and make my nights longer thereafter.

Near to his home in Bowmore he kept a small white boat which he ran to the fishing grounds of Loch Indaal. He had a fiddle which he had taught himself to play, and our last hours together were filled with strathspeys and reels and merry laughter.

John said: 'I was out in the boat one day when it struck

me what a lucky man I am. The sea was calm and the view clear. I had fish aboard and I knew that when I got home the dog would come to take my cap, and my little granddaughter would be running to meet me.

'I realized all at once that I was utterly happy and richer than any millionaire.'

I write about Captain John Cameron because, in a world fraught with discontent, he was the most contented of men. The sea taught him to be pleased with what he had, and not to hanker after what he had not. The stars laughed with him, for they were all kindred voyagers.

He was a man who mastered complexity and found perfect freedom in simplicity. He keeps returning with every cloud that passes.

10

A Few Interesting People

One of my great friends was Sandy Campbell, a large and lovable West Highlander who was one of the Clyde's senior pilots. He was a native of Kilchoan on the wild peninsula of Ardnamurchan. The sea surged in his blood and the Gaelic of his childhood came softly to his mouth. He was the gentlest of men.

His father, a sea captain, took him on his first voyage when he was fourteen. The year was 1914 and they were not many hours at sea when a U-boat surfaced and fired a shot across their bows. Clutching his pet Airedale, he took to the boats with his father and the rest of the crew.

He next remembered staring into the barrels of German revolvers, seeing his father's ship blown to pieces, the dreary hours adrift in the North Sea before being picked up by a passing trawler and landed at Lerwick in the Shetlands.

The experience did not spoil his appetite for the sea. He sailed the great southern oceans, marvelling at the rolling easterly swell, his kindred feeling for the wide-winged albatross, the golden galaxies of the stars at night. He lived for the sea and its traffic. He seemed the unlikeliest person in the world to become my golfing instructor.

We were quaffing pints at lunchtime one Saturday when Sandy suggested a game. I hadn't played since my pre-polio days and this became painfully apparent as I sclaffed my way around Clober Golf Course outside Milngavie.

I had to balance myself firmly on my caliper leg – the right. I had to be careful not to overswing the club: if I did, I would topple and give my famous impersonation of a falling tree. When I struck the ball I dared not transfer weight to my left leg because my knee would collapse and I would smite the ground with my ear.

Sandy studied my game with enormous patience. Picking me off the grass for the umpteenth time, he began to give me some quiet advice.

'Learning to hit the ball would improve your game for a start,' he said drily. 'We have let so many players through already that, at this rate, we will reach the eighteenth green about midnight.'

'And so what do I do?' I snarled amiably.

'Keep your head steady,' he said 'Rotate your arms around it. Keep your left arm straight. Uncock your wrists at the very last moment and let your club and arms follow through.'

I tried his recipe. To my astonished delight a sweet click enriched my ears and the ball flew, straight as a homing bee, for a thrilling 150 yards. Not only that, I was privileged to admire its flight from a vertical position. Ah, Sandy, what hours of pleasure your tuition bred! We will surely play again around Elysian greens, if our wings do not interfere with our rhythm.

Practice, of course, improved my technique. But golf, I found, was a painful game. By the end of a round my caliper had done its best to cut a groove in my groin. All the padding on earth could not stop it, and more than once I retired to the nineteenth hole with bloody pants.

I discovered that by adding a length of tube to my boy-hood driver I had a club with whiplike action. A three wood, two, four, six and eight irons and putter completed my equipment. I learned to hit a ball dead straight, but could never achieve a distance of more than 180 yards.

One day I took my problem to a professional. He watched me hitting twenty balls arrow-straight up the fairway. Not one of them broke that 180 yards barrier. The pro stared at me.

'You don't want my advice,' he said. 'You want a doctor.'

In my eagerness to better my game I approached a maker of limb appliances who, I had heard, could perform miracles for disabled people. He watched me waddling up and down, then said: 'If you can get your surgeon to agree to amputate your legs above the knee we could fix you up with much better artificial limbs.'

I was about to laugh when I suddenly realized that the man was serious. I politely declined his kind offer. Not even a great game like golf is worth such sacrifice.

Many of my newspaper friends were keen golfers. While their ambition was to keep on breaking eighty, mine was to shatter ninety – a feat which I performed only twice in my life. They were good enough, when we played, to give me a handicap and, of course, it should have been the other way round; for my mere presence on a golf course was enough to put any opponent off his game.

Playing once with Jack Coupar at Troon, I used my driver off the fifteenth tee, hit my second and third shots with the same club from the fairway, and was still 100 yards short. When I drove again and the ball clattered into the hole for a par four, Jack's immaculate game went to pieces.

At Littlehill, near Glasgow, I was being consistently out-driven by my colleagues Jimmy Adamson and Tom McCaffer when I made up my mind that, like it or not, I would pivot on my left leg as I drove.

I teed up, swung and transferred weight as I struck the ball. There was a sickening thud as my body hit the ground in front of the tee. When I sat up with ringing ears, Jimmy was rolling on his back in mirth, and Tom was staggering away to retrieve my club from a nearby wood. I discovered that I had outdriven them both by quite a few yards. It was my longest golf shot – well over 200 yards – and it swung the game in my favour, for during the rest of the round my opponents kept being convulsed with giggling fits.

Specialist shots came naturally to me. I think I am the only golfer to have pitched a ball *under* a green (it was being returfed at the time) and I once holed out from a bunker with my walking stick.

The more seriously my opponents took the game, the more my unorthodox style seemed to put them off. I was rarely in the rough as my shots were seldom long enough to reach it. As my frantic friends zig-zagged from hazard to hazard I would take the shortest route to the flag, utilizing every contour of the ground. I used a wooden club for short holes and putted from as far out as fifty yards. Speech play I did not find necessary: my unorthodoxy was more devastating than words. Had I offered Arnold Palmer a stroke a hole and restricted my weapons to driver, walking stick and putter, I might just have managed to stupefy him into defeat.

'If you can't join them, beat them' is a useful motto not only in golf. The amount of misdirected energy expended by the human race is incredible.

The answer to a loud argument is surely not a louder one: the most likely result of such an exchange is deafness. It takes a shaft of humour, a quiet rejoinder or sometimes even a splendid silence to let sense prevail.

I used to dread being asked to write what is known in the newspaper profession as a Powerful Piece, the big gun usually reserved for firing broadsides at inept government, social injustice or the manager of Scotland's football team.

Such an article is often as not so stiff with statistics, turgid with facts and groaning with opinion that its impact is like that made by an elephant tumbling into a pond. The displacement is huge and the shock waves enormous, but within seconds of the splash one realizes that the sight of a tumbling elephant is too funny to be taken seriously.

It was with a view to infiltrating humour and a little light relief into a rather ponderous subject that I was sent to one of Edinburgh's early International Festivals of Music, famous for their symphonic solemnity. My job was to write a daily diary about some of the interesting people in the city. There was no lack of material.

Edinburgh pubs were pimpled with minor poets lamenting in English the decline of the Scottish Lowland tongue, and complaining justifiably that Scottish culture was not being sufficiently represented.

Tyrone Power was in town, enjoying a reprieve from the transparent world of celluloid by appearing in a three-dimensional theatre. He received me in his hotel bedroom, clad in a shirt and dressing gown. He poured whisky while the sun was not yet above the yard-arm and talked about his ex-wife Linda Christian. As he spoke he kept fiddling with the diamond cuff-links she had once given him. Alimony, he said, was a terrible thing: it was costing him thousands.

Compared with my image of him as a screen hero he seemed a very soft tough guy. I felt sorry for him, and have since wondered if he ever sold his cuff-links before being claimed for the last Universal.

Emlyn Williams invited me to tea. He was giving a one-man performance of Dickens characters at the festival, and even offstage it seemed that he dare not for a moment relinquish his grip on the nineteenth century. He dressed like a Dickensian, spoke and even poured tea like one. In a crowded hotel lounge it was all a trifle embarrassing. Edinburgh housewives gawped and giggled. To the un-initiated he was more pixillated than Pickwickian, but his conversation was fascinating.

In my hunt for celebrities I attended cocktail parties, and there is no more diabolical invention. A cocktail party is a cross between a slow waltz and a mannequin parade, so loud with ineffectual chatter that you can't hear what people haven't got to say in the first place. For non-athletes like me it is purgatory.

As you enter the room your hostess is nowhere in sight. Somebody offers you a drink and you accept gratefully. You have now a walking stick in one hand and a glass in the other. Your hostess comes to greet you. Transferring your glass to your stick hand (careful) you extend your right hand to shake hers.

'Lovely you could come,' she says. She insists – simply insists – that you have one of her delicious savouries. You dare not refuse. You now have a stick and a glass in the left hand and a squadgy anchovy thing in the right. This is the moment she chooses to introduce you to Mr Shamduck.

So long as Mr Shamduck does not want to shake hands, you are all right. You can bow instead, spilling a modicum of sherry down a trouser leg or the skirt next to you. If he insists (as all Shamducks do) on pumping your handle you have several courses open. You can squelch the savoury heartily into his palm, you can pop it into your mouth and shower him with crumbs as you say 'how-do-you-do', or you can drop it into some convenient receptacle such as your glass, your pocket, or even his pocket. Remember that there are never any tables or chairs at a cocktail party – for the reason that they might possibly encourage people to sit down and hold an intelligent conversation.

Sir Thomas Beecham was in Edinburgh that year, conducting himself, his orchestra and the world at large with impish dignity. He had opened the festival with a performance of Sibelius Symphony No. 2 which one critic felt was unbefitting to a great occasion.

'The mountain laboured and brought forth a mouse,' he wrote. 'The mountain was the Edinburgh International Festival. The mouse was the second Symphony of Sibelius. . . .'

On the morning the criticism was published Beecham sailed into a press conference like a windjammer. 'Stand forth the man who called Sibelius a mouse,' he ordered.

The critic obliged, pointing out that it was the choice of work and not the composer which he considered mouselike.

'Then you ought to say what you mean,' boomed Beecham, and the scolding he handed out made me glad that I had not written the offending article.

It had struck me that Edinburgh's old Usher Hall might of itself provide the basis of an article. How many conductors, I wondered, had visited? How many great artists had gladdened its auditorium? I went along to talk to a hall attendant who had been there for many years.

We entered the green room where he spoke animatedly of the musicians he had met, their quirks and foibles. For some reason he wanted to show me the magnificent bathroom where many an artist had lain soaking and steaming away fatigue after an arduous concert. We were chatting happily there when we became aware of a presence behind us.

'What,' asked Sir Thomas Beecham, 'are you doing in my bathroom?'

I could, I suppose, have told him I was the plumber, but I trundled out the truth instead. Beecham stories were legion. He had the gift of a sharp wit suited to most occasions. He did not fail me now. Jutting his goatee beard, he said: 'As a journalist you should know that the paper here is privately owned.'

I fled slowly.

People have a habit of lamenting that the days of the great characters are past, but I am convinced that the process of creating them goes on undiminished. Of course, they take time to mature, like good wood and whisky, and most of them have a tendency to be fairly venerable.

The first I remember meeting as a child was in the Banff-shire village of Tomintoul. Mr Sim was tall, speedwell-eyed and wore a splendid waterfall of a beard which he called his white heather. I was allowed to stay up late to meet him because he was a philosopher, and my first question to him was suitably profound: 'Are there such things as fairies?'

He stroked his white heather, meditated, and gravely replied: 'There will always be fairies so long as there are good people to believe in them. I will take you to see some in the morning.'

He did too, conveying me over a shimmering, summer moorland in his pony and trap. Where a young burn tumbled through a glad dell we halted, and I remember the scent of myrtle singing in my nostrils, and flies singing descant to the psalm of summer.

'This is fairyland,' said Mr Sim – but I could see none of the inhabitants.

'You are not believing hard enough,' said the sage. 'You must use your imagination. Only when you do will the fairies take shape in your mind.'

I suppose this was my first lesson in science. It sticks in mind because never before, and seldom since, were there people around sober-minded enough to discuss fairies with me without sniggering and falling into the drunken torpor of what they call reality. Trees, houses, pens and books – things which you can see and touch – are contained by the third dimension. Fairies, or belief in the risen Christ, or looking forward to a birthday weeks ahead, belong to the fourth dimension of the imagination. This makes them more, rather than less, real. Possibly more people today than ever before believe in fairies, but they call them space-travellers, Martians or Daleks, wrapping them in scientific garb in an attempt to make them seem more contemporarily probable. I will always be grateful to old Mr Sim for helping me to see more clearly the things which are not always there to be seen, to understand more vividly that the present time is made up of events which have just happened, or are just about to happen.

Sir Harry Lauder was another character. If he overpainted the Scot as a kilted caricature with a thorn stick and moths in his sporran it was because the world wanted to see him in that guise.

Not long before he died he combined with my father in recording, for the BBC, some of the songs which had made him famous. Father, when he looked at them, was appalled by the poor musical grammar of their accompaniments. He sat down and re-orchestrated the lot. And Harry Lauder was not at first pleased.

'Young man [my father was in his forties]. D'ye realize I've sung these songs all over the world?'

'That's what bothers me,' said Father. 'You have – and the accompaniments were still terrible.'

To his credit, the old minstrel was big enough to accept this. His son John, killed during the First World War, had left behind a silver fountain pen, and this treasure, suitably engraved 'To Ian Whyte for Service Rendered' was presented to my speechless parent.

'It's leakin' a bit,' said the donor, 'but I suppose you could always get it sorted.'

Sir Harry arrived for his recording session with the orchestra wearing a cardigan which all but concealed his kilt. 'I love a lassie' was scheduled for performance, but age, alas, had dimmed the soloist's recollection of his own words. He faltered for a second but, great trouper that he was, carried on singing. 'Aw, God!' he carolled, 'the auld bugger's broken doon!' For years this priceless recording was played privately by BBC sound engineers. What a shame it is that such classics are liable to censorship.

At his home in Lauder Ha', Strathaven, Sir Harry had a room filled with the trophies he had collected during his world travels. He had casts of rainbow trout caught in New Zealand, and ornaments of gold and ivory from Africa and India. But he gave pride of place to a small slab of wood, pointed at one end and pierced amidships to accommodate a gull's feather.

It was inscribed, as I remember, 'Small boy's boat, discovered beside Loch Eck', and its second owner never tired of showing it off.

'There go a laddie's dreams,' he would say, seeing in his mind's eye the wind blowing on that feather sail as it crossed the dark waters. I think he associated the rude toy with his own dead son, and that it had much to do with 'keeping right on to the end of the road'.

Whatever sentiments islanders may hold for Caledonian MacBrayne, the shipping company, the character of its captains rates even higher than its freight charges. Sea and tide bred them, fed them, roughened them and softened them. Great gales had always greater Gaels to ride upon their backs.

'Squeaky' Robertson, he of the huge stature and high-pitched voice, became as legendary in the Minch as Fingal and the Norse sea harriers. I met him in South Uist, in the year that the bottle-laden SS *Politician* struck a reef and provided Sir Compton Mackenzie with the foundation for *Whisky Galore*. Like nearly everyone else in the Hebrides, Squeaky was in high spirits. When I asked him what was the most dangerous passage among the Western Isles he had to scratch his head for an answer.

'Och, well,' he said at last, 'from here to there is pretty easy but sometimes things get a wee bit difficult in between.'

Squeaky was present when a telegram arrived from the far south. The sender stated that he hoped to be in Loch Boisdale in two days' time 'By the grace of God – and Captain Robertson.'

'Och, aye,' said Squeaky reflectively, 'two good men.'

When the old 500-ton steamer *Loch Earn* plied no more between Oban and the Hebrides, and a brash new ship stood top-heavy in her place, I sought out John McInnes, captain of the old vessel, and asked him what his worst sea experience had been. Was it when he rammed the basking shark in the Minch and all the deck cargo hurtled for'ard? Or was it the storm when his masts kept kissing the sea on either side?

'Bad, bad – but no,' he said. 'It was the time we were coming from Tiree and the sea as flat as the floor below us.

We were entering the Sound of Mull when the fog fell like a blanket. You couldn't see a hand in front of your face.

'I came down to slow ahead and then stopped the engines. I blew the siren – *Bmmmmph!* – and got the answer back from the mountains – Bmmmmph! Closer and closer to Tobermory we drifted, and all yon beautiful, expensive yachts anchored in the bay. *Bmmmmph!* – Bmmmmph! Closer still . . . and then I heard it – the most terrible noise I ever heard in all my days at sea.'

'And what was that?' I whispered.

'The sound of the wee birds twittering in the bushes.'

Such characters may be rare, but finding them is often more rewarding than tracking down so-called celebrities.

At a party, held to lionize a well-known sportsman, a gushing woman assailed a colleague of mine with an equally well-known cliché: 'You journalists must meet a lot of interesting people!'

'Perhaps,' he replied, 'but certainly an awful lot of people meet a few interesting journalists.'

One of them was my old colleague John S. Clark. Few men, past or present, can ever have had a more full or varied career. In his youth he had been with a circus. Taming and handling the big cats was his speciality and he had a fondness for snakes commensurate with my own loathing of them. He had been a Glasgow councillor, Member of Parliament and, despite his Sassenach birth, was in his day the accredited world authority on the life and works of Robert Burns. When I joined the *Scottish Daily Express* he was occupying his latter years in writing a weekly column for children.

John's stories were fascinating. Thin, frail and bald, he would point to the livid scars on his head where Wallace, his pet lion, had clawed him, or display the marks on his hand where a python had bitten him.

'Poor old Wallace was only playing,' he used to murmur affectionately, producing the snuff box he had had made from the great beast's dew claw.

During his circus days a tiger developed toothache and became unmanageable. Its trainer demanded its destruction but young John intervened. He asked the circus blacksmith to fashion a pair of large pincers and, this done, advanced to the animal's cage. He requested two attendants to grasp him firmly round the waist while he presented himself at the bars as bait. When the tiger sprang at him John clamped the pincers on the offending fang and hung on.

'He thrashed about as I hoped,' said the doyen among dentists, 'and so pulled his own tooth. His trainer said I had ruined his temper – and so, of course, I had to make friends with the animal.'

Entering the cage, he sat down in front of the snarling, bleeding creature and began to make placating noises. Within half-an-hour his hand was ruffling the tiger's neck to the accompaniment of grateful purring. The trainer quit and John got his job.

If anyone laughed at his stories John would produce photographs. One showed him rubbing a leopard's tummy while a lioness held him aloft with her teeth clamped in the seat of his trousers. And just for good measure, he would sometimes bring some of his pets into the *Express* office.

He would borrow a lion cub or a monkey from Wilson's Zoo in Oswald Street and introduce them to our staff, and such were happy encounters. Less happy was his insistence that he could cure my horror of snakes by bringing me a live specimen to handle.

'Don't dare,' I warned him. 'I know they're clean, harmless, beautifully-marked, warm, dry and affectionate, but I can't tolerate the sight of them.'

I was at my desk one morning when John sat down beside me, clad in an old raincoat. Being busy, I didn't take much notice of him until our secretary began to make strange noises. Jean's face had gone white and her eyes were focussed on a point above and slightly to the left of my head. I glanced up and, for a split second, met the unwinking black stare of an anaconda. My piercing scream and sideways sitting leap brought the office running.

'He's only a baby,' John crooned. 'Come and hold him – he's quite beautiful.'

'Baby' was a full five feet long, had a head like a trowel and a flickering tongue, but somehow he managed to arouse the maternal instinct in some of our girls. Women, strangely, seem less repelled by snakes than are men. I have been told that this has something to do with their sexual make-up; that there is something about the serpent which some women positively enjoy. If this is the case, ladies, abandon your contraceptives, throw away your bras, belts and barricades. If you wish to obviate the population explosion in the world just coil an anaconda between the sheets.

We trembling males – I was not alone in my revulsion – ordered John to take his livestock away. He did – but not before the reptile had defecated on a chair usually occupied by my old colleague Magnus Magnusson. This tribute to a fine journalist, broadcaster and friend, we felt, was totally unwarranted. We fled down to the pub and ordered large whiskies. I was reaching a hand towards my glass when I noticed that the man standing next to me had on an old raincoat. . . . 'He's really a beautiful creature,' John's voice was proclaiming. The coat writhed and again we departed in haste, leaving our drinks untasted and deeply mourned.

One evening in the office I was unaware that one of Scotland's great law lords lay terminally ill in Edinburgh, or that his obituary lay ready to run. By some cruel chance I was alone when the News Desk phone rang and a colleague came on the line from our office in Edinburgh.

'Do you know about Lord "X" who's just dying?' he asked. Disastrously, the word I thought I heard was not 'dying' but 'died'.

'No,' I replied. 'I didn't even know he had been ill.'

'Tell the Desk,' he said, 'that we now know the cause – cerebral haemorrhage.'

I was already late for a meeting and left a note for the Night News Editor. 'Hugh Welsh phoned to say that the cause of Lord "X"'s' death was cerebral haemorrhage.'

His obituary was run as front-page news. Only when copies of the paper reached Edinburgh late at night was the disaster spotted.

A lot of best suits were being worn next day. The entire management had assembled, and I was placed at the end of the conference table directly opposite the editor.

Since initial responsibility for the calamity was mine, he suggested that I should set the ball of explanation rolling. I told him that I genuinely believed Lord X to be dead; that

Hugh's message had been to stress that the cause was cerebral haemorrhage. Hugh, in his turn, agreed that his telephone call had been to inform the News Desk of the nature of Lord X's illness, and not his death. In a tense room the essential difference between 'dying' and 'died' took on terrible significance. How my error had managed to snowball right through the newspaper process, no questions asked, provided thought for all of us.

Sandy Trotter was magnificent in his loyalty and generosity. I heard later that Lord Beaverbrook had demanded the rolling of one or two skulls, my own among them. I heard too that Sandy refused, threatening that, were any of us going to be sacked, he, as editor, would join the ranks. This was typical of the man and epitomized the spirit which made the *Scottish Daily Express* the mightiest newspaper of the fifties.

It gave us no comfort to know that a certain law lord had been intrigued to read a front page tribute to himself and perhaps muse, as did Mark Twain, that reports of his death had been an exaggeration.

11

Close to the Wind

The sea began to tingle in my bloodstream. I do not know why this should be so, since, so far as I know, there was no seafarer among my recent ancestors. But perhaps the reason goes deep into pre-history. We were once all creatures of the sea, gilled and similar, until we crawled ashore, struggled on to legs and finally stood erect, trying to peer back down the misty path of evolution. Perhaps something of the water-baby lingers on in all of us, bidding us sail round the world or merely paddle our feet in Millport Bay.

I was in Arran one blazing summer's day when I bumped into my friend, Jock Kerr Hunter, a man who has done more than most to promote recreational facilities in Scotland. I met him in Lamlash, that slumbering village whose chief occupation lies in watching important events like cloud change or gull activities. His lovely, dark blue yacht *Saionara* lay in the bay, and why, he put it to me, should I dash off to catch a palpitating steamer to the mainland when he was sailing in the morning?

Why indeed. We spent the hot, mellow evening yarning over drams, and the sun was as reluctant as ourselves to visit bed. A huge round-eyed moon rose over Holy Isle and stared at us in wonder. We rambled down to the jetty and, along with several holidaymakers, formed ourselves into a choir – no raucous chorus such as is heard on a Glasgow Saturday night, but a proper, orderly Orphean group. Old Alec Hamilton, 'Ching' to his friends, local shopkeeper and uncrowned king of Arran, came from his house to conduct us. He is the only man I know whose eyebrows, by colliding, become diverted to run the length of his nose. We sang Donizetti and Schubert and Psalm 23, and our conductor wept with unashamed pleasure. The local policeman, as I remember, came to move us on but stayed to sing, and from a faraway hill farm some querulous collie raised his voice in attempted harmony; but the poor animal lacked musical taste. On such a balmy, golden night as this there is no place I would rather be than on a Scottish island. Sleep is something which simply has to wait – until it rains, or unimportant trivia crop up, like opening shop or making money. Somehow we managed to tear ourselves away from Arran in the morning.

To keep out of everybody's way, I sat on *Saionara*'s deck behind the mizzen mast. The wind was freshening and we began to tack up the Firth of Clyde, bound for Largs. Unused as I was then to yacht behaviour, I discovered that *Saionara* sailed her fastest while lying on her side, an attitude which Jock termed 'gun'le under'. Perched athwart her tapering stern, I found myself getting very wet and in grave danger of falling overboard. My eye fell on a rope and, making sure it was fastened to a cleat, I tied the free end around my waist.

'You can trawl me for mackerel if you like,' I told Jock, 'but at least I'll know I'm attached to your boat.'

He seemed to consider this very funny at the time. The pity was that he omitted to inspect the rope to which I was secured. I was still tied to it when we put in to Largs. Quite a crowd was watching from the shore. Under the critical scrutiny of fellow yachtsmen, Jock was sedulous to make an efficient job of dropping sail.

'Down jib,' he ordered his crew. 'Down mains'l. That's it . . . now, down with the mizzen.'

Bodies rushed aft around me. As the mizzen fell a searing pain shot through my ribs and I was yanked half-way up the mast, there to dangle while our shore audience bellowed its delight.

'What the hell are you doing up there?' Jock howled at me. I was in no fit state to tell him that I didn't know a mizzen hoist from a bosun's braces. As the sail was raised again I thumped back down on deck, wondering if I looked like an hour-glass. Jock was pretty furious and I abandoned ship in deep disgrace.

One of Jock's crew, Alistair Galbraith, nicknamed 'Captain Whiskers', rowed me ashore. The beard which inspired his title enveloped his face and his eyes peeped through the tangle like those of a fox in a whin bush. He wept with laughter as he rowed. My ascent of the mast, he tee-heed, was the funniest thing he had seen in ages. Injured pride and ribs – and sheer spite – forbore my mentioning that he was on a collision course with a catamaran. When we struck, he fell flat on his back with his legs in the air, waggling feebly: he looked like an upturned, hairy spider.

It was hilarious landing, but a large whisky was required to free poor Jock's seized laughter mechanism.

Whether or not my misadventure had anything to do with it, he had *Saionara's* mizzen mast removed. The alteration made her even more beautiful, but I had not yet finished messing about with his rigging.

As an official of the Scottish Council for Physical Recreation – now the Scottish Sports Council – he had a small fleet of yachts available for charter, and *Saionara* was among them. Some friends and I persuaded him to let us sail her for a week. If he worried about my ability to cope aboard, he gave no sign. If he thought I was a little mad, he was kind enough not to say so. Our appointed skipper was Ross Kennedy, a former newspaper colleague and a sailor of experience.

We set off from Dumbarton one June day, left the shadow of the great rock and moved down the Clyde. I soon found I could get around a yacht fairly easily, and perhaps more safely, than many men with a full complement of muscles. Agile men sometimes have the habit of moving around on deck without troubling to hang on to rails or rigging. A sudden squall, and even the fanciest of footwork can not prevent a header overboard. To move about I *had* to hang on, never unloosening one hand until I had found a grip with the other. Handling heavy sail was beyond my strength, but I could steer a pretty true course, read a chart and do simple navigation. And I could cook.

I myself can live quite happily, like a dog, on one meal a

day; but my mates had the appetites of cormorants. One night I determined to fill their caverns to capacity. Into our small oven I put six steak-and-kidney pies, each a good nine inches in diameter, one for each man. Unfortunately I forgot to leave room for expansion, and the pastry rose like a rebellion, jamming the lot together in the oven, and I had to chisel them free as best I could. I served them with a Popocatepetl of potatoes and peas and prepared to receive compliments, but none were forthcoming. Puzzled, I bit into my own pie and discovered the reason. The manufacturers, I swear, had put cement, and not flour, in their pastry. How it defied gravity by rising at all is a mystery. We ate what we could, and it lay like ballast in our stomachs.

'Give the rest to Sammy,' someone suggested, and there was a chorus of approval.

Sammy was a herring gull, saturnine of eye and solitary in habit, who had adopted us as his mascot and meal ticket. He was bolder than the brass on the binnacle. He was not above invading the galley and filching the breakfast toast, and it was not his arrogance which annoyed me so much as the deposit he insisted on leaving behind in down payment of goods received. He was floating astern of us, as usual, when I threw him the last mortal remains of our dinner. He screamed in ecstasy. He gorged and gobbled, sipped a little sea water and guzzled again. Then, almost imperceptibly, he began to sink. His plimsoll line (or gull equivalent) slowly submerged. His seedy eye took on a glazed look. He was pie-eyed, someone said. He seemed ready to founder when he managed to expel a little air. Only a speedy digestion saved him from sinking without trace.

Next morning he left us in peace: he was probably too busy planning a bombing raid on a distant pie factory, and I hope that his unsolicited testimonial did not miss the mark. We sailed without him through the Kyles of Bute and into Loch Fyne. An enormous basking shark kept leaping abeam of us, and we were keeping a wary watch on him (a ton of shark through the rigging would not have delighted us or Jock) when the dorsal fin of a killer whale sliced the water only yards away. *Orca Gladiator*, they say, is harmless in Scottish waters, warmed as they are by the Gulf Stream;

but nobody seemed desperate to go swimming. Excitement seemed to tremble in the air that day.

We had planned to circumnavigate Arran and were rounding Pladda Light at the island's southern tip when a line of white tops showed in Kilbrennan Sound between Arran and Kintyre. The wind, when we found it, was about Force 4 from the north-west – a fair breeze to speed up the sound towards Lochranza and a hot meal.

I went below and put on a pan of mince to simmer, letting my bottom slide up the curve of her hull as *Saionara* heeled to port. We were past Carradale when a tremendous bang sounded above my head. The whole yacht shuddered, reared like a frightened horse and fell broadside across the wind. The pot of mince leaped from the cooker, clearing the fiddle, and cascaded through our living quarters in a boiling stream. Feet pounded on the deck above, and amid the uproar I could hear Ross shouting: 'The mast! Oh, my God, the mast!'

My first reaction was to slither aft through the mince to start the engine, and I was trying to coax it into life when someone tramped on my head.

'Leave the engine,' Ross was yelling. 'You'll only foul the prop. All our rigging's in the water.'

I was fairly shivering with bravery. Lockers were bursting open. Crockery crashed and bottles broke. Some unseen force kept thudding against the hull. I badly wanted to go on deck to see what was happening, to escape the claustrophobia which was stifling me; but I knew I would be more hindrance than help. I climbed on a bunk and managed to see through a porthole. The chaos outside was sickening.

Saionara's forty-foot mast had shattered off three feet above deck level, but by some divine providence had fallen overboard with all sail, and had not crashed down on my companions. But now its jagged butt was threatening to hole our side with every roll.

The hatchet, kept to hack away rigging in an emergency, had been swept away, and so had our boathook. My friend Mike Grieve was only just keeping the stabbing mast at bay with the nearest implement available – my walking stick. We were drifting southwards for the open sea, and we had no radio. There was a Very pistol aboard, but no cartridges. Compared with this predicament, the brutal safety of Islay's lifeboat seemed something of a luxury. I put on a life-jacket and wondered miserably if its buoyancy would be sufficient to support both myself and a steel caliper. But my mates on deck managed amazingly to free the rigging. They had mast, sails, shrouds and halyards wrapped up, and had towed this bloated bundle astern. And now the engine could be started, and we began to limp, dead slow, for Carradale, and we might just have made harbour with any luck, but at that moment a big bluff fishing boat came chugging to our aid. Ah, the blessed sight of her! She seemed the most beautiful boat in the world.

She hauled us in to Carradale's neat harbour, scolding us with the tut-tut of her exhaust. We tied up alongside her motherly bulk and wrung her skipper's hand in gratitude. We toiled up a steep hill to the hotel and burst in upon a crowd of astonished holidaymakers. Men in crisp summer attire and girls in chic dresses regarded us with some distaste, for in our relief at being ashore and alive, we had rather forgotten how we looked – or perhaps did not care. A fashion commentator might have done justice to our mannequin parade:

'Michael is modelling casual yachting wear in ripped wool and engine oil which contrasts nicely with his seaweed and blood accessories. Bill favours a beige jersey with matching mast-splinters and petrol-tinted plimsolls. For his ensemble Ernie chooses sloppy trousers, and a dark shirt to match his finger nails. Don's sweater of Shetland wool is attractively patterned with mince collops. . . .'

Mine host rounded the bar at the gallop, spreading out his arms as if to shield his clientele from our unlovely appearance. When we announced that we were shipwrecked stragglers, both attitude and atmosphere changed. From being ugly vagrants we became ugly celebrities. Everyone wanted to buy us drinks and ask us questions.

What had happened, and where, when and how? In a quiet village where even Monday's washing signals messages of interest, we became the event of the week. And all at once the legendary small world shrank even more. Mike's doctor, on holiday from Glasgow, rose to greet him. On being introduced, I discovered that his partner was my own G P. Bill met a friend he had not seen for years. Ernie embraced a mate he had served with in the R A F and had not seen since. Not even Ross was immune from this delightful infection; for Sandy Galbraith, our rescuer, remembered him as a small boy on holiday with his parents. All the ingredients were there for a gala night performance, and that is exactly what we had.

Half of Carradale, it seemed to me, trooped aboard sad, shattered *Saionara*. They came in relays to sit among mince and broken crockery. We drank and sang songs, and discused the deep and shining religion of the sea which embraces all men. How happy we were that night! We gave each other our lives to cradle and caress.

Mike had gone missing for an hour or so. He returned with a half-bottle and a strange tale to tell. He had made yet another friend, he said. They had entered a shop together, had passed through to the back premises and thence to a cave in the hillside. And there, in a cavern of joy, there lay such a store of whisky as would have kept ten alcoholics, or five Lewis crofters, happy for a month. Mike's genie had bidden him drink his fill, and Mike had not let him down. Even we could see that. But where in Carradale that cornucopia was situated he could not remember. Perhaps it was one of those fairy grottoes which men dream about, and discover only in the imagination. But where else, after midnight, could he have got the half-bottle?

We poured Sandy Galbraith a measure of fairy gold, and he felt moved to tell us the story of our rescue. It was scarcely less astonishing than Mike's cave saga.

Sandy had been sitting by the kitchen fire (he said) and had asked his wife for a glass of water. As she filled it she had glanced through the window which overlooked the sea.

'There's a bonnie sail going up the sound,' she remarked. Such a casual statement would not have stuck in most men's minds. Sandy leisurely drank his water and, some ten minutes later, rose to replenish the glass. When he looked from the window there was no sail visible. Other men might have shrugged and turned their backs, but he did not. He knew that a yacht, beating up Kilbrennan, could not have passed from view in that space of time. He took his binoculars and began to scan ten miles of sea. That sea was dark blue, and so too, you will remember, was *Saionara*'s hull. There she lay, about a mile out, scarcely visible without her mast and sails.

'I called my son-in-law,' Sandy said. 'We gathered the crew and wondered for a while whether to alert Campbeltown lifeboat. We decided at last that we'd go out ourselves . . . by glory, but that's a good dram . . . aye, and here we all are, sound as whistles.'

Dawn burst with a fearful crash upon a great communal hangover. A bleary sun rose shuddering over Arran. We packed our grips and prepared to travel by road to Campbeltown for the ignominious return to the mainland. The gulls jeered derisive insults at us and the old *Waverley*, last seagoing paddle steamer in the world, beat out some obscure moral with her wheels.

I rather dreaded facing Jock Kerr Hunter. I had visions of being re-christened Jonah and dispatched to the lesser mercy of a killer whale. Some old men I had known had sailed before the mast; but so far I had only sailed behind it, up it, and finally without it. I hoped that, given time, Jock might come to see the funny side of it all; and, being Jock, he did.

'Remember offering to let me trawl you for mackerel?' he asked. 'It's one hell of a pity I didn't take you up on that.'

Perhaps, on reflection, *Saionara* was ill-named; for it is an odd thing how the names of ships seem to influence their character. To name a ship *Titanic* was sheer arrogance. The *Queens* in their day were truly regal. The *Marie Celeste* suggests some ethereal insubstantiality. Even little vessels I have known seem to share in the relationship of name to behaviour. *Mischief*, which I sailed with my sons on Loch Lomond, was as fickle as a ferret, and I almost lost a finger in her jib winch. The great *Owl*, on which six of us voyaged to the Hebrides, spread vast soft wings and soared the seas. *Mairi*, the tiny sixteen-foot aluminium boat which Ross Kennedy and I sailed from Glasgow to Ardnamurchan, skirting the Atlantic, behaved like the lady who named her. *Clarag* –

'broad-beamed woman' in the Gaelic – bore us from Kyle of Lochalsh to Irvine like a lusty fishwife. You may argue that all this is pure fancy, but there must surely be a grain of truth in it, for my theory applies even to the human species. I have met Campbells with squint mouths, as their Gaelic name implies, Camerons with noses awry and MacGregors who thought they were the sons of kings. There is no law governing this: it is just something which happens often enough to be intriguing.

But I was talking about *Saionara*. And *Saionara*, translated from the Japanese, simply means 'good-bye'.

12

Down to the Sea Again

It might have crossed some minds by now that, while messing about in other people's boats, and even breaking them, I was not putting in a great deal of work. But it all depends on what you mean by work.

I can think of at least one victim of God's circumstance who stands for eight hours a day, five days a week (teatime included, overtime excluded) in a factory workshop, building a part of the part of an aircraft which was declared obsolete before even the plans left the ground. He does this for £50 a week, or perhaps £100, with the consoling thought that one day he may be made redundant.

I can think too of the underprivileged native, be he black, white, brown, yellow or beige, who lies under a magnolia tree in a remote area full of exciting wildlife, like rats, mosquitoes, rumours, revolution and leprosy, counting the petals falling on uncomputerized fingers. He does this for nothing at all in the happy consideration that one day he might be useful.

There is only one answer to life and that is to live it. After all one's lifetime happens so infrequently that it seems a shame not to enjoy the thing while it lasts.

Work, for a lot of people, means slavish application to a job which, to a greater or lesser degree, they heartily detest. They are the five-day masochists, the world's walking wounded.

Less dedicated are those who spend their working hours devising means of doing as little as possible for as much money as they can wring out of the company. They are the squabblers who demand a classless society – but at the same time classify themselves as skilled, semi-skilled or unskilled workers. The more skilled a man becomes, the less skilled he seems to be at doing anything other than his special job. He becomes like a machine tool. Take the job away and he is helpless. Like a machine tool he cannot adapt.

As I write, the world has decided that it has too many motor cars, and the world is probably right. A Scottish car plant has decided to cut production to allow sales to catch up. The workers are angry, for their lives depend on making cars. They demand that the management keep up full production of a commodity which, at present at least, fewer people want. The alternative is strike action, during which time no cars will be made (and no money) although the fume-laden world may breathe a little more freely.

Imagine a very healthy community whose doctors are told to reduce their numbers, and the doctors' reply: 'If there are so many fit people around that our services are not required, then we must make more of them ill so that we can make them better.'

The picture is ludicrous. But so seemingly are the laws of supply and demand, the inflexibility of labour and the muddle-headedness of managements and governments.

My father-in-law, who spent a lifetime in the motor industry, had a favourite story to recount. One day he received a letter from a wholesale firm.

'Dear Sir, how many cartons of vehicle sidelight bulb No. PQ/389 will you require for scheduled delivery next month?'

He replied: 'Dear Sir, thank you for your letter. As we already carry a sufficient stock of PQ/389 we will not require any delivery next month.'

Back came the astonishing query: 'Dear Sir, had you required cartons of PQ/389 to be delivered next month, how many would you have ordered?'

To many of my colleagues I appeared work-shy. All was well when I appeared in the office to dream up ideas, await instructions, twiddle thumbs, pop down to the pub, chat up secretaries and clatter out an occasional cadenza on the typewriter. So long as, like Chaucer's lawyer, I seemed busier than I was, no fault was to be found. I became TV correspondent, leader writer, music and drama critic, children's editor, diarist and features writer before achieving the ultimate and doubtful glory of having a column of my own. But office life bored me rigid. News did not grow there, unless piped in through the cold medium of the telephone. The office was for processing and marketing.

On real working days I went fishing, or talked to shepherds, or leaned on the moss of bridges to watch dippers dipping and wagtails wagging tails. On holiday or off, I wrote about the countryside, prompted, I think, by the instinct to survive in the first and last bastion of survival. And readers seemed to like what I wrote, and asked for more, and got it. And the more I wrote about what I liked, and felt to be important, the less I visited the office.

This was fatal to good relations; for there is a school of thought which teaches that if you are enjoying what you are doing you cannot possibly be working; and that you are not working until you are seen to be working – and being miserable into the bargain. It annoyed quite a few jealous disciples of this creed that the products of my idleness should find their way into print. It mattered not how long before dawn I left home, how long after midnight I returned, or how many calipers and cars I wore done, I was paid for being lazy. Some twenty-five years and 2 000 000 words later I am unrepentant.

Believing that I was a frustrated water-baby – or perhaps wanting finally to be rid of me – my superiors always seemed at pains to pick on me for awkward sea assignments. One morning I was sent to Greenock with the object of boarding the old *Empress of Scotland*, lying at the Tail of the Bank. Prince Tungi of Tonga, now king of those Friendly Islands, was aboard and I was required to interview him.

It was a straightforward matter to hire a launch and motor out to the tender which lay alongside the *Empress*. It was fairly simple to climb the tender's companionway and negotiate the gangway leading from her top deck into the white hull of the liner. Therein, a lift hoisted us up into the Royal presence.

The prince was enormous. How near to three hundredweights he scaled would have been impolite to ask, but his heartiness was at least commensurate with his stature. He was delighted to see us and led us to the cocktail bar, ordered drinks and talked volubly. So fascinating was his conversation (and so liberal his hospitality) that time fled unnoticed. A steward jolted us back to reality.

'I take it that the gentlemen of the press are going on to Liverpool?'

No, we were not. Why did he ask?

'Well, the tender has already left and this ship is due to sail in five minutes.'

We gulped, shook hands, said thanks, excused ourselves and made as graceful an exit as hurry permitted. Down in the lift we went, and along a passageway, and where the gangway had once stood there was nothing now but a rope-ladder.

Fifty feet below, our little launch bobbed hopefully. Vertigo, my old enemy, kept hitting me behind the knees.

'My God,' I said, 'I can't possibly get down there.'

'You'll bloody well have to,' somebody muttered, 'unless you want to go to Liverpool.'

One man took my stick, and another lowered me through the gaping, grinning door. My hands found the rope-ladder – but my feet did not. I clung there like a window-cleaner who has just taken one tiny, backward step. I don't think my feet ever touched a rung on the way down, and the further down I went the more that accursed ladder swung, dashing me against the *Empress*'s steel foundation garment. Ten feet from the bottom all strength ebbed from my hands and I fell the rest of the way. The thud as I landed in the launch knocked all the air out of me.

'Dear heaven,' a voice was saying, 'do you want to hole a good boat?'

By the time my lungs were reinflated I could no longer think of a suitable reply.

Never again, I told myself. But soon I was having to ask Sandy Campbell if I might accompany him down the Clyde. Somebody wanted an article about river pilots, and, of course, all eyes were looking in my direction.

'Don't worry,' said Sandy when I told him of my unsea-

147

worthiness 'it will be as easy as . . . pie.' I think he had been going to say 'falling off a dyke'.

'We'll board a petrol tanker at Bowling and sail down river as far as Gourock. When the pilot cutter comes out to meet us, we will just step from one vessel to the other.'

We sailed from Bowling at 6 a.m. on a freezing February morning. The iron decks of the little tanker were white with rime and the cold seemed to burn through the soles of my shoes. We were nearing the spot where the *Empress* had lain when the cutter put out to meet us. Lightning, I consoled myself, does not favour encores. Sandy and I stood on deck and watched the pilot boat gliding alongside, matching our speed.

'When do we stop?' I asked innocently.

'We don't,' he replied. 'We just step across when the gap narrows. Look, give me your stick [where had I heard that before?] and I'll go first.'

Timing things to perfection, he hopped smartly over a yard-wide chasm of icy green water. I stood petrified. Sometimes the gap narrowed, but more often seemed to broaden. The glaucous sea gurgled and giggled.

'Where's this tanker making for?' I called across.

'The Mersey,' Sandy said.

Ruddy adjectival Liverpool again. One day I'd really have to go there to find out what it is about the place which makes suicide such a sweet alternative. And as for lightning. . . .

'Just step across,' Sandy cajoled. 'We'll catch you.'

I stepped. Because the gap was widening again, I missed. I caught the cutter's rail with one hand and Sandy grabbed the other. But my legs were in the water, the February water, the nearly thirty-two degrees F-for-Fahrenheit water. They hauled me aboard like a limp cod and laid me out to dry or to die. That I did not do the latter was due in large measure to a large measure. Like any good West Highlander, Sandy kept in his pocket a half-bottle of medicine known to be efficacious in cases of frostbite, midge-bite, snake-bite and insomnia. In this instance one dead man ensured that Sandy and I might live. We consigned John Barleycorn's corpse to the deep, solemnly and with reverence.

It was not so much the braggart in me which led me into

accepting foolhardy assignments. Looking back now from a safer vantage point, I am fairly certain that fear was the spur. There was curiosity of course; and there was pleasure in looking back on a difficult job, done at least, if not well done, and that in itself was an incentive to carry on and tackle the next. But always, I think, I was afraid of failure, of refusing the challenge, of losing confidence and, perhaps worst of all, losing my job. Where would I find another? That question was always nagging at the back of my mind. I liked to think of myself as being pretty fit and active, but I knew that, come the crunch, I could not go digging ditches, felling trees or signing on aboard a ship bound for Rio (or Liverpool). I thought of going freelance, but friends who had done so advised against it: making the transition was a tough and often chancy business. And so I clung to security, afraid to bridge the gap between ships.

Things came to a head with the ending of the fifties and the arrival of a new editor, red-haired, breathing amicable fire, and bringing from the south that passionate fervour which the English seem to reserve for excursions into Scotland. He strolled around the office, chummy arms around our necks, uttering his dread warcry: 'It's a braw, bricked, moonlicked nicked the nicked!' – even in broad daylight. He claimed to know little or nothing about Scotland, but was determined to learn fast. And he did. The strange thing was that we, who thought we knew everything about our country, were jogged by his questing mind into the discovery of how little we really did know. One tends to take one's native heath for granted: the best explorers are usually foreign.

If this new broom did not sweep clean it certainly raised a lot of dust and cobwebs.

The Gaelic toast *Slainte Mhath* intrigued him – as did all Scottish drinking habits. Roger Wood enjoyed a full life. And since '*slainte mhath*' meant 'good health', and as some health and fresh air seemed necessary to lighten the darkness of politics and other disasters, he ordered me to start a column, light-hearted and connected loosely with Scottish conviviality.

'When do you need the copy?' I asked.

'Yesterday,' he replied, and this was typical of the man.

There are about as many tales concerning Scotch as there are Scots to relate them, but the only authentic one I could remember at the time happened once when I was in Wester Ross.

An illicit still was concealed on a certain peninsula, and in case it is still there, forgive the pun, the location shall be nameless. One day something went wrong with the apparatus. A new length of copper tubing was required to make a worm – the spiral coil through which the liquor distils.

The distillers were both MacKenzies, and this is giving nothing away for, as the saying goes in those parts, you have only to lift a stone to find a MacKenzie sitting under it. Anyway, the enterprising boys noticed, during their travels, that some copper tubes were lying handy up the Kerry River where the hydro dam was then under construction. One tube surely wouldn't be missed. The only danger was the vigilant eye of Winston Churchill.

That worthy was a Customs and Excise officer who, dressed in his uniform, so resembled the great man that his nickname will endure long after his real name has been forgotten. He had the habit of patrolling the district perched rather comically astride a small motor scooter. But it was said that he could smell moonshine ahead with a forty-knot gale blowing on his back. The lads had to be careful.

They stole up Kerryside in the dead of night and sneaked home unobserved with a fine length of tubing, and were so pleased with their success that they decided to celebrate with a modicum of the good home-made. And if you have tasted the stuff at all (as I did once, but only once) you will know that it has a kick like a backfiring bike. This was their undoing.

'Let's bend her into a coil before daylight,' said one.

'Using what for tools?' asked the other.

'There's a pole at the end of the garden will do just fine. We'll bend the tube round that and have a new worm in no time at all.'

To fashion a straight copper tube into a spiral without kinks requires both strength and delicacy, but the lads were equal to the task and made a perfect, even coil.

Winston Churchill was on his morning rounds when he

became aware of a subtle change in a familiar landscape. He was not sure at first what it was, but something was glinting on a roadside pole. I never learned if he finally recognized it for what it was, and I never learned if one Mackenzie cursed the other for choosing the wrong template, or blamed drink, or darkness, or both. The fact remains that when you wind a coil around a telegraph pole, the cross-trees stop you from sliding it off at the top.

The story became the first of a column which ran weekly for about three years. The freedom it offered was welcome, but the school of discipline was still in session.

A fleet of Russian trawlers had put in to the Sound of Fetlar in the Shetlands, and all Britain was agog. They might claim to have come to fish, but relations between countries had become exceedingly strained, and the popular impression was that they had come to spy.

Roger approached me casually one afternoon. 'Pop up to Fetlar and get yourself aboard a Russian trawler,' he said. 'Pretend you're interested in their fishing methods, but find out what the hell they're up to.'

Just like that. He might have been asking me to find out what film was showing at the Odeon. I scanned his face for signs that he was joking, but he wasn't.

I telephoned some contacts in Lerwick – men I knew to have had some dealings with the Red trawlermen – to discuss the possibility of boarding a 'spy ship'. I could hear their eyebrows lifting. Was I out of my furry mind? Was I looking for a free passage to Siberia? There was certainly nothing they could, or would, do to assist me.

Somewhat relieved, I told Roger, expecting this to be the end of the matter. I should, of course, have known him better.

'Get on to the Foreign Desk in London,' he ordered. 'Ask them to contact Moscow and arrange facilities for you.'

Dumbly I obeyed. It might titillate some minds were I to be the first intrepid Briton to board a Red trawler, but the risks involved seemed to outweigh any possible glory. I had daymares about being rowed out to a dark ship, about trying to climb a rope ladder under the surveillance of guns, about trying to explain my mission and conduct an interview in sign language, about being mistaken for a spy (well . . .) or even welcomed as a refugee from the dreadful capitalist regime. Nights in the Arctic. Fish and sick.

The Foreign Desk and Moscow could not help, and my pulse rate decelerated – for a few hours.

'Why aren't you aboard a Russian trawler?' Roger bawled, and I told him. 'Right. Send a telegram direct to Mr Kruschev asking leave to board a ship to study Russian fishing methods.'

I did – and our telephone operator made strange choking noises when I dictated the message to him. It was marked *Please reply. Urgent.* But the Russian supremo did not reply. I do not know if my cable even reached him, or whether my name went down in a little fat, black book in the Kremlin. There was silence.

'Why aren't you aboard a Russian trawler?' Roger shouted two days later.

'Do you want me to drop in on one by parachute?' I retorted.

'That's your problem,' he jeered. 'You've spent a week piddling around and getting nowhere. Are you scared or something?'

That did it. I blew up, told him where he could put his Ruski fleet, fish, funnels, fo'cs'ls and all, and sat down and wrote my resignation. When I thrust it at him he read it, laughed wildly, and tore it into confetti.

'Why aren't you aboard a Russian trawler?' he asked – this time without seeming to require an answer. He did not get one.

For Roger, the impossible was always attainable. Had I hired a frigate and boarded a Red ship by force I think he would have been delighted. Any international incident arising from the action would have been seen as grist to the mill. What's a war so long as we get a page one spread?

After this he left me in peace to get on with my column. *Slainte Mhath* became a useful weapon with which to poke bureaucracy in the ribs, and puncture consciences, and intrigue tourists, and fight the depopulation of Highlands and Islands, and combat industrial waste and pollution, and champion wildlife. I was writing about good health, and enjoying good health. I was married with three healthy children, and I was happy. And I should have remembered again the danger of allowing oneself to be too happy. Always, always there is the plunge for which one should be prepared. One should restrict one's happiness a little, reef it in a little as if it were a sail.

It came as a profound shock to be told that my father, as much brother and friend to me as parent, was dying of lung cancer and had only a few months of music left.

13

Finale and Prelude

Father had, in fact, about six months to live. For him, perhaps, those moons rose and set too quickly, but for those of us closest to him they dragged across interminable skies. We were told that on no account should he be told the nature of his illness, and many times since then I have wondered about the wisdom of such advice.

Many of Father's friends were doctors, and medicine was a subject which greatly interested him, not out of morbid curiosity, but because he liked to know how the human body functioned. As the pain in his chest increased, and breathing became more difficult, he would ask outright if he had cancer of the lung.

'Of course not,' we would lie. 'It's just a stubborn virus which is taking a long time to clear up.'

We guarded him like watchdogs, fearful in case a whisper of the truth should reach his ears from some outside source. The strain was pretty terrible. When he began to receive radium and cobalt treatment he again asked the dreaded question, and again we lied. He seemed to accept this. And then, as his illness progressed, we began to suspect that he *knew* we were evading the truth and that he himself was joining in the deceit to save us embarrassment. I think he finally knew what his trouble was, but he and we played out the façade to the bitter end.

Would telling him the truth have shortened his life? Or would it have awakened some inner strength in him to battle on for longer than he did? And would that longer battle have been unkind? Was our lying kinder than the truth? I have asked these questions many times and know that there is probably no answer to them this side of yonder.

At the end of September, when the mists were whisping in the yellow reeds, we went fishing on a small loch in Dumbartonshire.

'Well,' said Father cheerfully, 'let's make the most of it. This is the last day.'

'The last day of the season,' I corrected, lightly, in case he had meant something else. And Father grinned like the boy he always was.

Not before or after that day have I seen such a rise of trout. They rolled like little golden porpoises on some enchanted sea. They flashed in the sun and took everything we offered them. We were supposed to limit our catch, but on such a last day of days what men could have laid their rods aside? For those were surely Galilean fish, destined by some new miracle to reach our net. We laid them lovingly in fronds of green fern and let their colours sink into memory through our eyes. We lit a fire of sticks on the bank and watched its blue smoke rise like a benediction, and felt the flames lap against our hands like puppies' tongues, and brewed tea, and laughed at silly things like coots and water hens.

'What a perfect day,' my father said. But the sun was setting. Autumn withered into winter and another year began. It was January when someone remembered that never in Father's lifetime had a recording been made of him extemporizing at the piano, perhaps his most unique talent.

Something had to be done for selfish posterity, but we dared not raise questions in his mind.

I cajoled him into attending a Burns Supper at the hotel owned by my wife's family in Irvine, there to play the Immortal Melody as a complement to the usual Immortal Memory. Ill though he was, he agreed. He did not know that I had a friend with a recording machine hidden behind a screen. Around a simple Scots air he built a lacework of notes that quivered like raindrops on a spider's web. The surface tension in that hall was almost unbearable, but nothing broke, or splashed.

He had not yet quite done with music. Towards the end

he was writing a mass for the Catholic Church and, at the same time, a piece for the Protestant faith (his own).

'This won't do, you know,' he said one day. 'I've let the Catholics get two bars in front of the Proddies.'

It was now March 1960. Even although I knew that the end was imminent the shock of his death was tremendous. The rivers stood stock still and the birds froze in the trees. For the first time I realized how much I had depended on Father. Physically I had managed to achieve independence, but even unconsciously I had seemed to rely on his authority, character, humour and common sense to shore me up. At the age of thirty-three I discovered I had a lot of growing up still to do. The next two years were pretty rough. My own marriage began to crack and finally crumbled. I tried to lose myself in work and to some extent succeeded. But always, at day's end, I had the feeling of drifting rudderless and without an anchor. Some men I knew seemed to thrive on bachelorhood, but I was not cast in their mould. And yet I balked at the thought of marrying again, forsaking the frying pan, as someone said, in favour of the naked flame. But that was before I met Anne.

It was an old friend from school who introduced me to this young woman with the burning desire to become a journalist. I thought she didn't have much chance, and said so. She thought I was abominably rude, and said so. And then, having got all the pleasantries out of the way, we discovered that we had quite a lot in common. We had both had polio at the age of twelve, and that was good for laughs. We adored animals and some people. We loved music, home cooking and vile puns, logs on the fire and houses that looked lived in, rudimentary golf and basic stories (provided they were funny). We found we hated politics, fat men, thin women, spoiled children, do-gooders, humbug and industrial disputes. Suffice to say that after fifteen years of laughter, few tears, and falling out mainly to fall back in again, we are as contented as pelicans on a fish farm. I count it an enormous stroke of fortune to have met her when I did.

From that moment on the rivers began to run again, and all the frozen birds suddenly burst out singing in the trees.

14

They Also Serve

I had been playing table tennis with a friend one night, too long and probably none too wisely, and when I wakened the next morning my joints creaked like rusty hinges and I ached all over. Getting to work was very painful, and the first person I bumped into was my opponent of the night before.

'Hullo,' Jimmy hailed me. 'How are you this morning?'

Grimacing bravely, I replied, 'To tell you the truth, I feel absolutely crippled.'

He stared at me for a moment and then collapsed in help-less laughter. I couldn't for the life of me see what was so damn' funny, and demanded to share in the joke. But it was some time before he could control his mirth. It was the word 'crippled' which tickled him so much. It seemed to him incredibly funny that, after so many years, I should only now be recognizing a fact about myself which he and every-one else had known all along. But this, of course, was not what I had meant. It was only when I looked at myself through his eyes, as it were, that I saw how ludicrous my remark must have sounded.

I had never really thought of myself as a cripple in the true sense of the word. It took a pulled muscle, a sprained ankle – or a surfeit of table tennis – to make me feel anything out of the usual. There was a further occasion when I men-tioned to friends (without thinking of the consequences) that I had athlete's foot and tennis elbow. I really had – but the only sympathy I got, thank heaven, was another gale of merriment.

One of my press colleagues had struggled all his days with a bad stammer. Relaxed, he spoke with fluency. But in moments of stress his impediment took full command. On an afternoon of office panic, when I was in a great hurry, he approached me to ask some question or other. Impatience must have shown on my face, tensing him up, for all he could utter was a long ululation of 'Ahs'.

'Look,' I said, 'I'm in an awful rush. You'll have to wait five minutes while I finish my copy.'

When I had done, I returned to him, full of remorse. 'I'm sorry I was so rude,' I apologized, 'but I simply didn't have time to listen to you. We both have similar problems when you think about it. I'm slow in getting anywhere on foot, and you sometimes take ages to say what you want to say.'

I happened to lean heavily on my stick at this moment, unaware that a scrap of paper lay between its rubber ferrule and the slippery floor. There was a splendid crash as I fell full length. Jack hoisted me vertical in his arms and grinned happily.

'Ah – ah – ah – there's just one difference between my problem and yours,' he said.

'What's that?' I asked.

'Mine doesn't land me flat on my arse.'

The fact of the matter is surely that every single one of us is handicapped. Babies and old people are handicapped, thalidomide children and the deaf and dumb. And so too are prize fighters with buffeted brains, and absent-minded professors, fat men and ugly women, alcoholics and total abstainers. All men are handicapped, but some are more handicapped than others. The trouble is that the architects and planners of our society are not yet sufficiently alive to the need for a broader view of the situation. There is always the danger of creating a norm, based on the false conclusions of statisticians. To find that the average household in Ardluck contains 1.95 children is an affront to spinsters and two-child families alike. It is simply not true. There is no such thing as an average family any more than there is such a thing as a normal family. You cannot therefore design things for normal people: the aim should be to make more things which can be used by everybody.

Take a simple invention – the doorknob. Its presence in my house presupposes that I can grasp it with my fingers, turn and pull. And because all 'normal' people can do this, it has become an almost universal household fitting. But is it universal enough? A man with palsied hands, or no fingers, or no arms, cannot turn a doorknob. Should fire break out in the room he is trapped. Sound legs or even teeth will not effect his escape.

But fit an old lever-type handle to the door and see how the picture changes. You can tilt it down with your heel, elbow, shoulder or head to open your prison. Even an intelligent dog can do this – and so can a mentally handicapped designer with 'normal' hands. Here, then, is a fitment which nearly everyone can use. It does not come into the category of special equipment and costs no more, perhaps even less, to produce. I do not suggest that any law be passed making lever handles compulsory. I mention them only as an example of how thoughtful planners can cater for a wider range of users.

In some of my earlier cars I could sit with outstretched legs, rest my heels on the floor and roll my feet (I cannot lift them) from one pedal to another. Any racing driver will tell you that this is the most comfortable way to drive. But among modern cars, other than some sports models, I have yet to find one whose pedals do not stick out like stalagmites. Any car I buy now, at least within the tolerance of my bank balance, has to have its foot controls adapted. Racing drivers and people like myself seem to be in a needless minority.

I raise my good fishing hat to the planners who instal lifts in public buildings at ground level. But my blood fairly boils when I see some old heroine stranded because the lift is an inch or two narrower than the gauge of her wheelchair, or because a lame-headed architect thought that two small steps would look pretty in the foyer. It took a long campaign by a gallant Edinburgh lady to convince the authorities that ramps should be cut at intervals in the kerbs of Princes Street to let wheelchairs (even prams!) cross the thoroughfare. Intelligent town planners might have thought of this in the first place, helping a number of people and saving some extra expenditure, not to mention needless frustration.

Steps and stairs are unavoidable in a world where living space becomes even scarcer, and provided they are furnished with handrails or banisters they can be tackled by many disabled people. Several times in my life I have cocked a leg over a banister and slid down (first ascertaining, in the interests of posterity, that the rail in question was not decorated with brass studs). Where there is no hand support one goes up and down stairs on one's bottom. Descending to breakfast in a hotel in this manner often leads old ladies to suppose that one spent the night in the cocktail bar, but the only alternative is to stay trapped or perhaps fall from the bedroom window.

When I look back on thirty-six years spent in the company of polio I must say in honesty that the experience has frequently been painful, frustrating and embarrassing. By far the worst is the embarrassment. When a friend of mine takes me sailing, he clips me into safety harness to lower me into his dinghy, and this has the effect of straightening my crooked spine, and hurts like the very devil. But pain is something one can learn to tolerate. There is some frustration when we reach the slip and I find I cannot walk on a skid-pan of wet seaweed, or climb the steps in the sea wall. But frustration and impatience can be curbed and controlled. It is when Joe hoists me on his back and tramps his way to easy ground through a crowd of strangers that I suffer agonies of embarrassment. And this is something I have still to learn to conquer. I will sail again, of course, and the same thing will happen. I will beg to be put down and allowed to wait until the crowd disperses. And he will tell me not to be so silly. I vow that never again will I allow myself to be made an object of curiosity, a spectacle. But there is always the next time. The rustling of a green sea swell, the beckoning finger of a far blue island, are matters clamouring for urgent attention.

Looking back, I find that there are no real regrets hanging around. I have lived a full life and I am nearly certain that without polio to laugh at me from the sidelines I would have missed something of the essential quality of living.

Some men require Everests before them, or voyages round the Horn to fulfil their sense of adventure. For those less fit there are lesser mountains and seas from whose summits and wild acres the view is every bit as rewarding. If it is merely to boast that you have been there – like sending a picture postcard from Plockton – the journey seems pale and purposeless. If it is made to test some fibre or other, to add a fraction to the knowledge of mankind, then the effect is worthwhile. The more you demand of life, and take out of life, the more you have to replace. This is simply the application of a good farming principle. Nothing saddens me more than seeing disabled people without the opportunity and, more important, the determination to join in the great adventure of living.

Some years ago I was in Forfar, assigned to write an article on the centre there which trains dogs to guide blind people, and also teaches blind people to work with dogs. I was prepared, I think, to write some awful guff about deserving causes – that which falls automatically to the bottom of every editor's tray – when a big yellow Labrador rose from under a secretary's desk and came to sniff at my feet.

'Hello, lass,' I said, patting the great lump. 'What a fine dog you are.'

A slim girl, sitting at her typewriter, smiled in my direction. 'Good morning, Mr Whyte,' she said. 'Mr Forrester is expecting you.'

I was astonished, for I had never seen this girl before. She turned her ear towards me, listened to my silence and interpreted it correctly.

'You're wondering how I happen to know you,' she said, 'but you telephoned yesterday to make an appointment with Mr Forrester. I recognized your voice when you spoke to the dog.'

This friendliness and secretarial efficiency stemmed from her blindness. The realization jolted me, and in the seconds it took me to recover, she was again miles ahead of me.

'Is this Mrs Whyte?' she asked the perfume hovering next to me. Somehow I managed to stammer introductions, but words are almost unnecessary in the presence of such supersensitivity. Alma was sad that our approaching footsteps had told her we were lame – but weren't the Angus hills lovely that morning? she said – the hills which we knew rolled russet and purple through her imagination, the hills which she had never seen, the familiar hills which we had still to see, clearly and without the obstruction of eyes.

'Come on, Scotia – coffee time,' she sang to the dog, and walked, fur in hand, unerringly to the door. And at the foot of some stairs the dog, nose against her knee, told her to be careful, and they trotted off together through a world of their own making.

Bob Forrester, in charge of the dog training centre, had no trouble in convincing me of the value of dogs in the therapy of the blind: Alma of the hills had said it all for him. It only remained for him to fill in a few details. He told me about the dog in Edinburgh which, on being told it was Thursday, would trot by herself through crowded streets to collect her master's pension. He told me about the Labrador whose senses were so exquisite that she could pick up a dropped needle from the floor with her lips, and place it in the hand of her sightless mistress. The fact that the training of guide dogs is expensive, and dependent on public subscription, made me determined to do what I could to help.

'Why don't your wife and you take a puppy for initial training?' Bob asked. 'You would keep her for a year and teach her obedience and good behaviour, how to walk without pulling on her lead.

'You would accustom her to traffic and industrial noise, show her what life is all about and give us back a poised, confident animal fit for advanced training.

'You would have, of course, to be brave enough to part with her at the end of a year,' he added significantly.

Anne and I looked at each other. We already had a Labrador and a young cat. Our ability to walk any distance was diminishing with the years. To add a puppy to our menagerie seemed crazy, but the world was suddenly full of people like Alma, and we knew that we could not refuse.

Life became more interesting. Cambus, a cream Labrador, was three months old when she arrived in our household, with a vast appetite and ears to match. Those ears, when she galloped, clapped together like pigeon's wings and folded over her eyes like curtains when she slept. Her tastes were Catholic. Books, chair legs, and the choke lever of my car were as acceptable as the cat's fish or Brandy's bones. Once, and only once, she used the cat's tail as a teething ring, the resultant fistful of hooks in her nose dissuading her evermore from repeating the experiment. It was our two older animals, and not ourselves, who first taught her manners, and gradually a delightful relationship grew among them.

At night Anne and I would walk her, teaching her to match our slow pace and not to tug against the lead. And behind us our old dog Brandy would amble, and behind her again the cat with his mizzen raised, speeding up occasionally to make sure he would not lose us. We must have made a strange procession, and sometimes, as we passed, people would stop and stare, and mutter, and hurry on furtively.

I thought that, in the interests of her future owner, Cambus should learn to retrieve such things as slippers, collar and lead – articles which Brandy knew by name, and would fetch when bidden – and lessons were in progress when an extraordinary thing happened.

The cat, who had been observing this game of fetch and carry with wide eyes, pounced on a crumpled ball of paper, brought it to me, laid it at my feet, and sat gazing at me hopefully. When I threw it he brought it back, and the habit, when he was not otherwise engaged in washing his shirt or working out the square of 43, became engrained in him. One January night, before a great storm played havoc in the west of Scotland, he retrieved a starling, unharmed and almost unafraid from the garden, and laid it at Anne's feet.

Cat and dogs looked on indulgently as it perched on her knee and screamed for the remnants of dinner – the fat from lamb chops, runner beans, cold potatoes to follow, and a sip of milk. After dining, our guest settled down to sleep inside the collar of my polo-neck sweater (which I happened to be wearing) and I suppose I ought to have turfed him out, but I think that I felt flattered.

I have seen, as you have, starlings rise from the fields in dark concerto, wheeling and lifting as a leaderless entity, and dipping down to roost like black foliage on the skeleton trees of winter. I have seen them extirpated from Glasgow window sills by workmen with steam hoses. I have seen them in our

Calderpark Zoo, hopping between a tiger's paws and picking up the peanuts thrown to him by his human audience. I have heard them called a plague and a pest, but who was I, when a millionth part of their number came snuggling against my neck, to deny it refuge? I telephoned to the RSPCA expecting to be laughed out of countenance. Instead, I found a kindred spirit.

'Let me finish my tea and I'll come straight down to you,' said a voice in the accents of my native county. And Inspector Ingram was as good as his word.

'It's a strange thing,' he said, examining the bird. 'It isn't damaged at all, but it doesn't want to fly. Why your cat didn't kill it is a bit of a mystery too. Anyway, I'll take it with me and let you know what happens.'

Later that night the storm broke. Chimney-heads crashed and trees toppled as a freak hurricane scythed across Scotland. But one starling roosted securely in an aviary. In the calm of a new day the inspector released him. And for days to come, when starlings whirled overhead, we felt we had restored a featherweight of balance to the flywheel of the world.

Training Cambus proved much easier than training most of the public with whom she came in contact. It was simple enough to get her to sit down on command, but well-nigh impossible to restrain the 'clever doggie' brigade from tempting her with titbits, asking for her paw, and generally countermanding our orders to her. Even to explain the purpose of the exercise was to invite such comments as: 'Aw, what a shame! Doesn't want to be a blind dog, does she then? Come and have a toffee, there's a good girl.'

Such sentiments are voiced by the people who give Britain the reputation of being a nation of animal lovers. They frequently buy their children a puppy for Christmas irrespective of its breed or potential size. When the kids tire of it, it becomes something of a nuisance. But to have it put down, or even neutered, they argue, is unspeakably cruel. It is much kinder (and easier) to give Lassie the freedom of the streets. When thousands of unwanted animals are put down every year, our nation of dog worshippers is horrified, but seldom self-critical.

Right through her puppy training Cambus, Anne and I weathered the storm of 'animal lovers', learning to spurn sweet speeches and biscuits alike. We had to do it – for at the end of the line there was a blind person waiting to be led from confinement into such an environment, full of scents, temptations and coaxing voices. Only a dog which recognizes and obeys one voice above all others can resist such pressures. And Cambus showed promise of being that kind of dog.

At the end of a year we wrenched her out of our hearts and returned her to Forfar for intensive training. And months later Bob Forrester telephoned.

'She's magnificent,' he said. 'She's one of the best we've ever had. She has met her new owner and they're training together now.'

All that finally remained to be done was to have Cambus spayed, for no blind person can be expected to cope with an animal in season. The operation was over and training had resumed when Bob telephoned again, his voice bitter with disappointment.

'Something odd has happened. Cambus won't go near a butcher's shop. The moment she catches the scent of one she puts tail between legs and flies for her life. She'll never be of any use now.'

It was a sad disappointment to us that such a fine dog should fail so near to success. I believe that somehow she had associated the smell of blood in shops with her own operation. But all was not quite lost. Articles which I had written about her and her training had stimulated wide interest. Money poured in from people all over Scotland – more than sufficient to train another dog; and I was present one glad day when this Labrador was introduced to her blind owner, a girl whose home was near to mine.

I watched it lead her along the pavement, warn her of the kerb, and cross the street only when it was clear of traffic. I watched it steer her wide of an overhanging hawthorn branch which would have swept her hair. And as if that dog had been a shower of rain, all the petals in that girl's face burst into blossom.

Cambus stayed with us for some years, filling the void

165

when Brandy died. We even managed to cure her of her phobia, but by then she had forgotten the refinements of her Forfar training. We were at pains to keep her occupied, encouraging her to fetch and carry for us.

We considered it her right, as it is the right of all domestic creatures – they who are in some ways more disabled than ourselves – to share the dignity of service, the pleasure of participation.

15

Three Times to Meet

On a day of summer heat when the road was shimmering and simmering, and the cone of Ben Lomond, that loveliest of mountains, seemed to melt in the haze, I took a friend into the inn at Gartocharn, the village which lies at the southern end of Loch Lomond. The bar was crowded and we sighed because Scottish licensing laws took little cognizance of summer.

Our policemen, on a hot day, have a dispensation to abandon their tunics and go about their business in shirt sleeves. But we Scots are not encouraged to carry our ale outside, to sit in the sun absorbing it, with the scenery, and enjoying the quiet conversation such civilized behaviour inspires. It is our lot, summer or winter, to drink behind closed doors and opaque windows. We must not be seen drinking in case we disturb the eternal slumber of John Knox. We must not express our enjoyment by singing, for drinking is a serious pursuit. We must gulp to leave time for another round before curfew bell. Our drinking laws are enough to drive us to drink, and we dream of a day to come when relaxation of the rules enables us to become sober, sensible people.

At a small table a woman sat with her husband, each with a half-pint, sipping carefully to make the beer last. The woman was strikingly handsome with the calm eye and high cheekbones which proclaimed her to be what, in my youth, was called a tinker, and has now been euphemized to the term 'traveller'. Glasses empty, they fumbled in purse and pocket and assembled a small scattering of coppers, too little to buy more beer. I ordered two pints and had them sent across.

The woman beckoned us to join her and looked at me gravely. 'You are very kind,' she said. 'You will sit down and talk with us.'

It was more a polite command than a request, and Bill and I sat at her table. Her name was Elizabeth MacDonald, and even in shabby clothing she managed to maintain an air of queenly serenity, and her conversation flowed easily, like a slow river. It led our listening ears through fields and dappled woods, bewitched our noses with the scent of wood smoke and pans of wild stew, and filled our inner eyes with aspects we had not seen before. Her husband sat silent, nodding agreement now and again, but allowing her to speak for both of them. Theirs was a hard life, brutal sometimes, but this was said without rancour. The countryside was theirs, the good sweet water and the clear air, hazels and willows for weaving baskets. Above all else there was the great, restless craving always to be on the move, following the seasons. But how sad it was that the people who lived in houses could not understand, and sometimes would not tolerate, their chosen way of life. She spoke simply and plainly, and, because she did not labour to impress, the impression bit deep. When we rose to go she held my eye and said a strange thing.

'We have met once, but we will meet three times before it is all over.'

Summer green mellowed into the ochre time of hairst, bread in the awn and stubble to follow, barren winter after that, and then a year or two during which the name of Elizabeth MacDonald tiptoed silently to the back of my mind.

And then one dismal autumn day trouble came to Peel Glen, behind Drumchapel. Some of that housing scheme's more enterprising younger citizens, time hanging heavy on the hands, invaded a tinkers' encampment in the glen and shot some of their dogs. It was an ugly situation in an ugly place, and I went to find out the facts of the matter.

Anne was brave enough to accompany me, and required to be; for, as we drove into the encampment, a crowd of sullen, silent men grasping sticks surrounded the car. When I got out and reached for my own peaceable stick I could see all the brown knuckles whitening. I was busy rehearsing my opening speech when a tall woman stepped from the doorway of a bivouac and stood like a queen among the tin cans and buckled pram wheels. She moved her hand and the men drifted away like shadows. And, heavens, was I glad to see her! And this was the second time of our meeting.

She looked at Anne and said: 'You were a little girl when you took ill and became lame. I remember how distressed your mother was, and I was very sorry, because your mother was a kind person. She did not turn me from her door.'

Anne stared in wonderment and so, I think, did I, for there was an aura about Elizabeth MacDonald belonging as much to fairyland as to the mortal world in which we stood.

To me she said: 'You have come about our dogs. I am not angry with the young men who killed my children's puppy. I am just sad that there are people who could be so cruel.'

The dogs, she said, had done no harm. She and her people had no quarrel with the townsfolk. They went to the city only to sell baskets and sprays of decorated hawthorn, but trade was poor because so many of those articles were being made by people in homes for the disabled and, goodness knew, they needed money even more than travelling folk. She and her kin would never have come to Peel Glen but for the fact that their children had, by law, to receive education. But if shooting dogs were part of schooling, she felt that the children would be better off under the gentler scholarship of the countryside.

Compassion surged in this woman like a sea tide. Her sorry dress seemed only to enhance her natural dignity, and I stood there seething with cold rage at a society which cleans its windows, but not its conscience; lusts after money, but not real values; acquires some literacy, but scribbles vulgarities; preaches love, but practises hatred; examines its leaves and scions, but forgets its roots; accepts complexity with a reluctant sigh, but sneers at simplicity.

And here this woman stood, without anger, among the rubbish of our own making (for it is we who choke the burns with our town trash, and her kind who go there gleaning).

By saying very little she seemed to say almost everything. She had known the love of man and the pain of mankind. She seemed to understand the simultaneous equations of birth and death, self-satisfaction and self-denial, music and silence, the spoken word and the dumbness which is poetry only to poets. I think she knew how the owl mourns the vole, and how the vole exults when her talons pierce his skin.

I think that she stood at the grey doorway of our coming and going seeing, however dimly, the other side of the great mirror through which we all must pass. But, as she said, I have to meet her for a third time before it is all over.

If I do not go around Scotland searching for her deliberately it is not because I am particularly superstitious or afraid. If I see her trudging under the eternal shepherd mountains of Glencoe, or camped among wild hyacinths on the road to Aberfoyle, I will stop and talk with her, and even if she should come seeking me on a cold day when the sun is dim, I will not hide from her. One must never hide from the simple dignity of humanity, or be afraid of it.

I am afraid of Socialism and Conservatism – or any other-'ism' which fetters the true spirit of humanity. I am terrified of anarchy which is the very antithesis of freedom, the outcome of misrule, the vandal child of careless parents. But I am not afraid of the human values which exist despite, and not because of, politics. I am not a very political beast, possibly because I have a flair for seeing two sides to most arguments, but the only road I can see clear towards the solution of our social problems is a return to a simpler way of living, a return to the soil which nurtured us, a reappraisal of our heritage.

Agriculture, I believe, is the mother of all cultures. Only when you have ploughed, sown, reaped and returned to the earth what you took from it can you afford to sit down and have a ceilidh, which is Gaelic for a party. The traditional songs of Aberdeenshire – the bothy ballads and corn kisters – were inspired by agriculture, and so was Beethoven's Sixth Symphony, and so was much of the poetry of Robert Burns. Grain is the very kernel of music, and the best performances are never achieved on an empty stomach. Neglect of the land seems a crime worse than suicide and not far short of murder, and I say this in bitter shame, looking at the town garden which I can no longer properly cultivate.

The tragic face which Glencoe wears, even on a day when the sky is blue as a hedge-sparrow's egg, has little to do with a silly massacre which happened there in 1692, and less to do with the tear-stained faces of the mountain judges on their everlasting bench. It has almost everything to do with those patches by the roadside, always a little greener than the rest of the glen, which mark the passage of ploughshares long ago. And you see, strewn in their midst, the boulders of homesteads again scattered on the land whence they were garnered, and rowan trees planted beside crumbled doorways to keep away witches – but defenceless against the factor's men as the people were cleared from the land to make way for sheep, as the heyday of the landlords began.

After the defeat of Bonnie Prince Charlie at Culloden in 1746 there was nothing for it but to punish the naughty, rebellious Scots by banishing them overseas, proscribing the kilt, silencing the pipes, and reseeding the scattered clan estates with feudal overlords from England. Grouse, deer and salmon became the playthings of the new aristocracy, and Queen Victoria took Balmoral (the climate suited her sickly son) and there she designed her own tartan, revived clan loyalty, and piped men out in regiments to the cornerstones of the British Empire.

The moaning drones of pipes, keyed rudely in A major, were heard in the Crimea and in South Africa, in India and along the Mediterranean shores. Their wild music roused weary limbs into action and bewildered our enemies for over a century as the Scottish soldier, ancestral sins forgiven, was marched from battlefield to battlefield. But in all that time there was no upsurge of grain in Glencoe, and that is the real tragedy. The ghosts of the dead who linger in the mists of Aonach Eagach must now gaze down in wonder on the fine road which ribbons beneath them, a long thin field which was ploughed and levelled, and crowned, not with oats or barley, but with a dark skin of asphalt which is not known to propagate. There is no bread in Glencoe. There is only the murmur of the bread van, passing through a wilderness were people used to eat.

Today it is industry which eats into the land and draws young people from the land with the lure of higher wages. And it is seldom the poor land which the power station or steel complex commandeer. It is the good land, drained and cleaned of stones by farmers for many generations. It is industry which breeds ugly towns, crime and petty vandalism, waste, pollution and an appalling disregard for the countryside which labours to produce our food.

At an agricultural exhibition staged in Glasgow's Kelvin Hall, I was admiring a young Highland calf when a city child of nine or ten years tugged at his mother's sleeve and cried: 'Hey, Maw – look at the big dug!'

'That's no' a dug,' she said, 'it's a coo.'

The deep irony of this is that 'cu', pronounced the same way, means 'dog' in Gaelic, a language old as Latin or Greek, which perhaps her grandparents spoke, and which is now struggling for survival in the Highlands and Islands. If the Gaels are fighting a losing battle it is not through apathy alone. As island schools close down, and Gaelic-speaking youngsters go to seek a living on the mainland, the sweet tongue of their youth tends to become diluted and lost in the hubbub of the city. Theirs is the language of fishing, crofting and weaving, themselves dying crafts, and only the revival of these industries, or kindred industries, will induce the young to stay at home.

Tir-nan-Og, land of the ever-young, has a hollow ring today, for it is the old who remain there, too weary perhaps to cut peat and tend the croft. And vacant homes are snapped up by refugees from the rat race of the remorseless, roaring towns. They too tend to be elderly and uninterested in or unable to treat, the land as anything other than a sanctuary.

A dozen years ago Anne and I holidayed on Skye, the isle of wings, and came under a spell so powerful that we could scarcely tear ourselves away. We talked poetry and sang songs with gentle people whose heritage went deep among the roots of time. We drifted at midnight in a boat on Loch Dunvegan while eagles brushed across the moon like moths and seals tumbled in the golden lane below. And we marvelled that 10000 Norse settlers had once won a living along this enchanting shore where now only a scattering of people remained.

On a hot Sunday I sat on a rock, stripped to the waist and sketching the distant Cuillins, and quite unaware that the minister was passing on the road behind me on his way to church. Whether he imagined that, because my back was bare, the rest of my person was in like condition I do not know. But one of my friends returned chuckling from the service with the information that his reverence had mentioned me in his sermon. I felt rather flattered – until told the context.

'And there is one among us in Dunvegan [he had intoned] who has the temerity to bare his body naked to God's fresh air, even on the Sabbath Day.'

But not even the rigours of a Skye Sabbath could quench my love for the island. I could have bought a croft house there for a pipe tune, let alone a song. I could have trimmed my lamp there, and burned peat, and gone fishing on a sea of amethyst and emerald, and learned a little Gaelic and a lot of wisdom. I could have written there, far from the square, hypnotic eye of the little telly god. But I could not have tilled the land or hacked my fuel from the fibre of the moor. I might have employed someone to do those things for me, but being a landlord, however small, in a place once bereaved by landlords, did not appeal. I might have laid my load on another man's back, but I knew somehow that the land would reproach me. Unlike Yeats among his nine bean rows, I would not have had peace there.

I drove across the Fairy Bridge and headed home, blinking like fury because I knew that Anne was crying by my side, and knowing that the web was broken, the happy trap unsprung, but that we were not at liberty to be free.

There are some 500 islands around Scotland's ragged 10000 miles of coast, most of them uninhabited, a few inhabited and many crying out for rehabitation. I have visited perhaps eighty in my time – or at least passed them closely and slowly enough to sense their aura and feel their strange, sad magnetism. I have sailed through the Gulf of Corrievreckan and felt that terrible sea cauldron wrenching at the helm and hurling us out into the Atlantic to land us on the paper-white sands of Oronsay. And there I have known that same soft hand upon my shoulder, compelling me to stay for at least a fraction of an aeon. I have felt it among the green woods of Islay, and on the brown isle of Barra where cuckoos make a clock factory of summer, and I have felt it many times.

I have been rowed into the cathedral which men call Fingal's Cave when the great diapason of the deep was roaring organ tones among the colonades, and making mockery of Mendelssohn, and I know that heroic men once rode this same sea surge, Kismul and Brecan, creaming the swell with thrusting prows amid a galaxy of islands. I know that some great Hebridean Odyssey was sung here once when there were strong voices to sing and minds to remember. But the islanders were scattered, and the saga broken by the wind and sea until now only dim snatches and fragments of it remain as thin echoes on forlorn shores.

I am not, however, pessimistic. I believe that there will be a return to the islands and to the neglected soil of the mainland. I believe there has got to be, for there must come a time when the spread of industry pushes our country, and others, to the brink of endurance, when every scrap of fertile soil is utilized for wheat and not for motorways, for potatoes and not for steel, for cattle and not for forests.

I believe that another greater agricultural revolution is due in which poor land will be revitalized and fish farms established; in which waste organic matter may be turned to useful methane gas, and the draught horse is again put in his rightful place before the plough. I believe there is a future for the windmill and the spinning wheel, the canal and the water wheel. And if this smells of putting the clock back then at least the expedient is better than having the damn' thing stop altogether. For this is a complex age in which the child is father not of the man but of the machine.

There are comptometer operators who cannot count, and graduates who cannot spell, and young philosophers who cannot reason, and young women who cannot cook for fear the habit might be catching, and so destroy their bid for liberation. And behind them there is a vast army of indifferent performers on electronic instruments – 'Oh, baby, as the ape in the zoo, with eyes so blue, said to you – yeh

174

yeh, yeh . . .' – whose incitement to frenzy is equalled only by its output in voltage, volume and vigour. Cut off all the power and energy, and only the cleverest among us will remember the basic ingredients for survival. Technology can improve our world, but it is not a world in itself, and it cannot supplant the seeds and the seasons.

Those wise enough to have listened to their rural elders know the pleasure evoked by the word 'home-made'. It describes jams and wines and honey cakes, wedding gowns and bootees, pink and blue. It embraces furniture and fishing rods, slowly made and reluctantly finished because the maker could not bear to take his hand away from the dusty silk of fine-grained wood and mummify it in varnish. There is always delight in savouring things home-made, in wearing them and using them; for somehow the love the maker put into their making becomes an intrinsic part of them. And that is their distinctive quality.

A greenheart rod, eleven feet long and fashioned in one sweetly-tapered piece, was put into my hand when I went to fish the Tweed for salmon. Frank Binnie, my old boatman friend, had made it, and the small Blue Charm he tied to my cast was also a child of his brown fingers.

'Throw your flee six inches from the bank of yon island,' he directed. 'No, no, no – six inches, no' six feet – tut, tut . . . aye, that's a bit better. . . .'

It was May, and for weeks no salmon had been caught in the swift run at Tweed Mill. But the sky came down to dance on the brown river, and warblers sang in aisles of apple green, and I was too deeply in love with everything to be prepared for combat. The little Blue Charm swam downstream. The jerk, when it came, nearly yanked the greenheart from my grasp. A fish like a silver quarter moon rose and set and lunged across the pool, and the reel screamed in ecstasy. Sky, river, trees and salmon all cavorted in the drunken sea of my adrenalin. How splendidly that fish fought – and how persuasively that wand in my hands soothed his temper! And then he sank down deep to sulk between boulders, and from there I could not shift him.

I wanted Frank to take the rod, but he would not. I gave it to my second-cousin George, but he could not move the fish. I tried again and, after half-an-hour, told Frank he'd simply got to take over.

Reluctantly he did, bracing his old back and bending the rod into such a vicious curve that suddenly an ominous creaking and cracking noise sounded beside me.

'Be careful of your rod,' I warned him. 'Never mind the fish.'

'That's no the rod creakin',' he grimaced. 'That's just the *arthreeties* in my spine.'

But he moved that salmon from the river bed, handed the rod back to me and netted the fish when I guided him ashore, and laid his lovely shape among the buttercups, and put his weight, accurately and without a balance, at fifteen pounds.

Two more salmon of ten and eleven pounds recognized a novice when they saw one, and quit the river to inflate my pride and bring about, of course, the inevitable fall. My own back, unused to such violent combat, collapsed and sent me to bed for three weeks as punishment – one week, that is, for each fish caught.

But one remembers the pleasure and forgets the pain. The learning is more important than the lesson, and I have gone fishing many times since, and will go again and again, until the last reeds shiver and the river and the sky become as one.

When water seems to come chuckling through my study, or loch waves mutter in my mind, I sit down and tie a fly. Its wings will be fashioned, perhaps, from the feathers of the pheasant we had at Christmas. A tuft of fur from the cat (he does not mind), a strip of tinsel, some thread and wool from my wife's darning bag, a dab of her clear nail varnish, and the job is complete. And there is no common Butcher or Greenwell, Heckham or Peter Ross, comparable with this nameless wonder. It has no title, for its pattern is never constant.

It is like a natural insect I have seen, or think I have seen, or even think I will see. And I take this tiny pioneer to the Lake of Menteith, where men have the good sense to farm trout, and set him about his business.

I cast him down the fringe of calm and ripple before the questing nose of a rainbow trout, and if the fish likes him it will lunge, snap and leap, flashing all the colours of sunset, escaping the net sometimes, but never eluding the finer mesh of memory where contentment lies.

That I taught my son to fish and tie a fly pleases me, and to think that he may one day teach his sons those arts pleases me more. For a machine can no more tie a fly than it can shoe a horse, or thatch a roof, or change a baby's nappy. Tools may help, but it is fingers which stimulate the craftsman, weave willows into baskets, dreams into reality and liking into work.

It may be that I am fishing when I see Elizabeth Mac-Donald for the third and last time, walking quietly down from the roadway, through the dark green alders on the lonely shore. I think that it would be pleasant to meet her there where the grey wagtails flicker like flames among the stones. And I like to think that there may be time left to talk, to tidy up the loose ends, to watch the lavender deepening in the sky or, better still to watch the sun rising on new hopes.

She may go on ahead of me, of course, or forget our tryst – but I really do not think that she will. Somewhere out there under the stars she is waiting, like truth, for the right time to keep her appointment.

16

Ladders in the Sky

On that day thirty years ago, when Tom Hetherington flew over Dollar in his dive bomber, and the starlings fell in fright from the apple tree among our teacups, and I resolved that if I couldn't join them I'd beat them, dreams of flying burned in me. I felt almost leprous with envy.

Tom, I learned, had decided to fly up the main school driveway between an avenue of trees simply, I think, to prove that it could be done. He had set his course on target, and was zooming in at something like 150 knots, when the thought occurred that the wingspan of his Barracuda was rather in excess of the gap between the trees. With no time left to pull up and over, he brilliantly decided to tilt wings and skid through on his ear, as it were. He was lucky to make it, missing the school flagpole by a whisker, and leaving it drumming reprimands in his slipstream. The nonchalance with which he recounted his adventure served only to make my green eye greener still.

I believe now that my desire to fly had nothing to do with winning a war. It was power which mattered then – power to impress, to explore and dominate, or simply power, if my truth be told, to compensate for limbs that would not function.

Bader, I remember, had legs when he learned to fly. Well, I had legs of a sort, and so why not? I volunteered to join the school Air Training Corps, and was turned down flat. I dropped broad hints to RAF friends that I would like to be taken up, but neither hints nor I ever were. Ten years were to pass before I flew (a mere passenger in the clinical tube of a turbo-jet airliner) and a further ten before I was allowed (briefly) to handle an aircraft, and by that time rude experience had rather dulled my appetite for the sky.

I was on a flight from London to Prestwick one evening, sitting next to the emergency door, where they like to put people like myself in case of flood, when a gorgeous red sunset began to suffuse the sky. I was admiring it through my starboard window when the thought suddenly struck me that, as we were flying north, the sun had no valid business to be setting in the east. By leaning forward I could look further back through the glass, and what I saw I did not like.

'This is your captain,' claimed a box up front. 'Please extinguish cigarettes and fasten your safety belts. We have developed a slight electrical fault and will be landing in Manchester.'

Our 'slight electrical fault' was manifested, I could see, by a tongue of flame trailing lustily behind the starboard inner engine. Most of my co-passengers were Japanese, and by looking at their faces I could see that cold fear is the same in Japanese as it is in English. I fastened my cigarette, stubbed out my safety belt and tried to fold my stomach neatly. All conversation in our sealed tube had ceased, but there was no visible panic. Every lurch and sway of the aircraft took on a new and dreadful significance as we began to lose height. An air of curious detachment seemed to fill the cabin. We were no longer human creatures, free to make our own decisions, and the thought was sickening.

And then came the yelp of tyres on tarmac, the gripping of seat arms, the slowing down, the clamour of fire engines, draught from an open door and cool rain – blessed rain – and, for an instant, a sense of anti-climax, the strange feeling of having been cheated. Exultation followed, a few sobs of relief from women with children, a gale of excited chatter and a charm of grinning faces. Happiness, like fear, is the same in Japanese as in English, but by then the sky and I had fallen out of faith, one with the other.

It was necessity rather than choice which took me off the ground from time to time. When duty called me to the Outer Isles, to Orkney or the Shetlands, I would have preferred to travel by boat every time, weather be damned. But a journal hungry for news does not have time to wait while its servants crawl like happy snails across the blue parts of the atlas. Either I would fly – or stand down to make way for a braver man, and since a knotted stomach is always preferable to loss of face, I flew.

Scraping past the cliffs of Sumburgh Head to land on the Shetland mainland did nothing to ease my apprehension, and experience of a bursting tyre while landing on Benbecula was far from reassuring, and my fear of flying reached a climax one dark December morning when I was due to board a plane for Dublin.

Anne came to see me off at Glasgow Airport, and when my flight number was called I found myself in the company of a whole rookery of nuns and priests, plumaged in black, and looking as merry as asbestos candles on a Christmas cake.

'Well,' said my wife cheerfully, 'at least you're in good company.' I gave her my best Sunday smile and set off across the tarmac, feeling that I was trailing in the wake of a wake, and wondering if it were at all possible to be limping to one's own funeral. A pretty deceptionist greeted me at the top of the scaffold steps and led me to my accustomed seat of penance at the door marked 'emergency'.

'You'll be much more comfortable here,' she lied sweetly, and left me to count my personal aids to gracious living – puke bag, life jacket and anti-panic brochure.

'This is your captain,' intoned the box up front; but it was to a flight commander of superior authority that my co-passengers seemed to be devoting their unswerving attention. And after the folding of hands, the crossing of breasts and the fluttering of rosaries, the fastening of safety belts seemed rather superfluous. Because of fervant entreaties, or perhaps despite them, we became airborne, leaping from cloud to cloud; but I knew little celestial joy.

Due to a vibration of the aircraft, a small screw attaching the ashtray to the arm-rest of my seat began to work itself loose. Before it could drop out altogether I used my thumbnail – the only tool available – to drive it home again; but it was not long before the confounded thing was jiggling out again. In that pious cabin it began to fascinate me, and it prompted the awful thought as to what might happen if a similar little screw were up to such mischief out there in the raving, inaccessible engines.

You can take such nervous problems to a doctor, but all he does is to offer you a soothing pill, and tell you that, statistically, flying is the safest form of transport. Or you can get so stupidly drunk before take-off that vital experience becomes a blur, a blot in the memory, or you can resolve not to fly at all. But these measures are mere palliatives, lanes of escape, and you must at last come to grips with the enemy and, even if you cannot vanquish him completely, at least show him a flash of temper.

Some months after my return from Dublin, that city so preoccupied with fine literature and leisurely funerals, I happened to meet an old university friend, Jamie Hunter, who had flown with the Fleet Air Arm, and was now stationed at Scone, where crowned kings never flew, teaching air skills to embryo pilots.

'What you really want to do,' he lectured me, 'is to lug yourself aboard a light aircraft with an instructor and learn to feel with your own hands how a plane responds.

'I'll fix up a flight for you. You'll find that flying is easier than driving a car, and you'll love every minute of it.'

Had I been nineteen instead of forty I might have agreed with him with more enthusiasm, but I could not very well turn down such a chance. Nasty as the medicine might seem, at least it appeared to offer the opportunity of a cure.

A thin blizzard was blowing on the morning I drove to Scone and sleet seemed to dribble in my veins and trickle down my spine, 'and perhaps', that insidious little voice was whispering in my ear, 'all flights will be cancelled, one in particular.' But at the second busiest airport in Britain (only London outnumbers its take-offs and landings) the morning programme was proceeding smoothly. I was introduced to my instructor, Gordon Lockhart, 'G' to his friends, and he armed me across slippery grass to where a small Cessna single-engined monoplane stood rocking wings in the February wind.

Jamie was there to heave my legs aboard and offer some last minute advice: 'Don't loop the loop if you can help it. It

isn't the weather for aerobatics and, anyway, the wing tends
to come off. . . .'

G gave me a brief run-down of the controls and also gave
my feet a passing glance. 'I'd keep them clear of the rudder
bar,' he advised. 'They might just get things jammed up –
besides, we won't really want much rudder today.'

When he got a clearance from the tower he opened up
full throttle and bumped us up into the leaden sky, trimming
tabs while I was busy adjusting my immortal soul. At 2000
feet he levelled out and took his hands from the control
column, and his voice crackled through my head-set.

'She's flying by herself. Take your own control and feel
how easily she responds. Turn the wheel left and we'll bank
round. . . .'

I turned, as one would guide a Mini around a hairpin
bend, and wondered why I was lying with my ear against
cold glass, and why the earth had tilted to such a crazy angle.

'No, no,' G crackled. 'Turn gently. You're not in a car,
you know. Feel the plane. Feel the response. Feel that you're
flying.'

And so I felt, twenty years too late perhaps, but with joy
and gratitude for all that, what it is like to fly a plane. To
the ways of ship on sea, serpent upon rock and man with
maid there must, I think, be added the way of plane in sky.
I felt the moth-like sensitivity of aileron in air, the bite of
the propeller's pitch. I felt the unseen places in the sky
where there is more air, or less air, the galloping of sixty
horses through a vast, ethereal field filled with invisible
potholes and ditches, and spanned by fences and hedges
there for the leaping. I felt the wild delirium of thrust and
counter-thrust, and even fear fell away with a soundless
scream to crash somewhere on the patchwork quilt below.
And yet, at that zenith of attainment, where humility should
have taken over, it was ambition which gripped me.

I was annoyed that a juddering façade of instrument
panel, peppered with dials, should obstruct my view. It
seemed quite unjust that a bafflement of science should
stand between me and a beloved landscape. Accordingly, I
moved my control column forward until much of Perthshire
hove into sight. And there was the Tay winding ahead of me,

and curving among its woods; and there were the foothills of the Grampians . . . and then there was G's voice in my ear asking: 'Are you watching your airspeed and altimeter?'

I was not, for I had rather forgotten where they lived among that great rash of instruments. And I am grateful to G that he hauled us out of a power dive on Dunkeld Bridge at 125 m.p.h. a speed beyond which, they say, wing and fuselage like to separate, and gave us opportunity and excuse to drink another pint together. And may it be forgiven that I swaggered a little in G's mess that day and felt, without having given the matter thought, an extra cubit added to my stature.

I knew then that I had done about everything I had ever wanted to do. I knew, and heaven knows, I could have led a less selfish life, but I doubted, and still doubt, if many men enjoyed a happier one. I would have to admit, I think, that, given the chance to play the tune all over again, I would like to do so without the syncopation of polio. And yet, in some strange way, I think that without it life would have been duller and more scant of pleasure and adventure. Without it I think I might have become a sort of athletic cabbage.

Flying was not in my mind when I returned, nearing middle age (whenever that may be) to Aboyne, the town of my birth, and there one pleasant Sunday I sat talking with my friend Donald MacAulay. He was going gliding over the Moor of Dinnet that afternoon, he said, and I remembered how some months previously a glider had crashed in the Dee, killing its pilot. Apparently, Donald said, he had blacked-out during an aerobatic manoeuvre. It had been a great tragedy, the more because gliding was such a safe and pleasurable sport.

And then I heard somebody asking if he might be taken for a flight, and realized that the speaker was myself, and heard my wish being granted, and heard my wife and nineteen-year-old son muttering the word 'mad', and wondered if they might not, perhaps, be right.

As in a dream that afternoon I found myself being strapped into a glider cockpit beside a kindly young man from Aberdeen University. Someone attached what looked suspiciously like a clothesline to our wide-winged craft, while the other end of the rope was tethered to a small red biplane. I heard its engine flutter into life, and watched the line draw taut, and felt the bumps as we skidded over rough grass and heather, and felt my stomach stay earth-bound while our glider, almost incredibly, lifted off before the tow plane had left the ground. And when at last he rose ahead of us the line slammed taut again, and up the Dee valley we flew, dipping and swaying and waltzing in his wild slipstream.

'When we reach 2000 feet we'll cut loose,' my companion said. 'Until we climb above that level I'm afraid it will be pretty bumpy.'

My own half of the controls leaped and shuddered between my legs, and we seemed to take an age to reach the desired altitude. We did not know until later, thank God, that the plane, lurching ahead of us, was having carburettor trouble. And then at last, when the altimeter needle touched the 2000 mark, my young friend pulled a yellow lever, and tow rope and plane both fell away and left us alone in the sky.

The wind against us was about Force 5 and our airspeed dropped to zero. We hung in the September air like an eagle, and when we banked to gain some speed we fell down some awful hole in the sky, and staggered up again to seek the standing wave of wind blowing over Lochnagar, the wind of uplift, the wind of sheer survival.

To those who stare up from the earth a glider is an object of grace, the very epitome of poise and calm. But to fly one in a mountain wind, before achieving the great peace which lies above the wind, is not for the faint of heart. The sensation is akin to rough water sailing. The wings flap slightly: if they were completely rigid they would break off. The wind buffets and blusters, and there are as many holes in the sky as there are pores in a large lemon. And again, while take-off from an established glider field is sweet and simple, there is no absolute guarantee that one will return to the point of departure.

That my companion did not pilot me to the calm above the wind was attributable more to my cowardice than to any flaw in his flying skill. He rushed me down my valley, and turned, and dipped down, and the green grass rushed up like a mother to greet us, and I saw my wife and son waving as we skimmed in low as the swallow skims, and I waved back. The thump as we hit the ground cracked my head hard against the cockpit cover, and only my good fishing hat saved me from a worse headache. And then there were 'well-dones' said, and the feel of strong, warm hands around me, and life was suddenly better than it had ever been; for up there in the thin under-heaven I had known a moment of clarity, a crystallization of understanding.

I had looked down on the most native part of my native land spread below me, field, moor and forest, as if some giant Highlander had laid out his kilt to dry among the hills. There was the yellow of corn in it, the mauve of ling in it and the deep green of pines, and through its warp and weft there ran the blue and silver thread of Dee. And I had seen Mount Keen again, where the fountain of childhood seemed to spring, and had traced the Tanar's wild glen down to where a cottage still stood among tall trees. And on its lawn I had glimpsed a child of six, outgrowing a romper suit, a child scared once of wings like ladders in the sky, and bereft of a toy glider, but looking up now with greater assurance to the man who soared above him.

And I had seen then, quite clearly, as one sees a trout flash in a clear pool, that fear is not invincible, that simplicity, the cornerstone of freedom, is not unattainable, and that the real wealth of man may be measured not in terms of his possessions, but by the things he can afford to do without.

A great optimism seemed to well up into me from the rich soil of my strath, and with it a sense of reawakening, a resurgence of faith in the future. And I heard again the Dee, the river of my youth, murmuring in her immortal valley, and I knew that as long as clouds touch hills and rivers run to the sea there is no end to anything but only a beginning.

Index